I0477922

Cover design and layout

Bee Kiong Goh
beekiong@gmail.com

This book has been designed using images from Flaticon.com

Collected Articles:

Research Samples *for* Business Management Degree Courses

Jun Yew Goh

TABLE OF CONTENTS

PREFACE

This book is based on research writings submitted as an undergraduate of University of Wollongong Malaysia KDU (UOW Malaysia KDU) from 2016-2020.

It is hoped that this collection can serve as a useful guide for research and research writing for those embarking upon Business Management Degree Courses.

Jun Yew GOH

Setia Alam, Selangor, Malaysia
23 September 2024

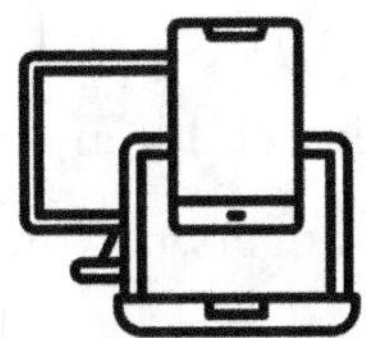

ARTICLE 1

Children should be given *unlimited* access to gadgets so they won't fall behind in technology.

To what extent do you agree or disagree with this statement?

Introduction

The controversial debate on whether gadget usage should be unlimited for children or not is relevant nowadays because of the craze among parents to give children gadgets to play with. They fail to realise that giving gadgets to young children is not appropriate. Often, they end up regretting when their children suffer from slower development rates, addiction to gadget usage and a variety of other problems (American Academy of Pediatrics, 2017; Astri, 2017; Margalit, 2016).

This essay discusses why unlimited gadget access is harmful for children, and therefore, worthy of control (American Academy of Pediatrics, 2017; Astri, 2017; Margalit, 2016). My stand on this question is in support of control instead of unlimited access. In discussing the title of the mentioned statement (American Academy of Pediatrics, 2017; Astri, 2017; Margalit, 2016), I will first mention one positive impact and then counter that with a discussion on how unlimited gadget usage affects children's physical activity and security and its impact on child development and family bonding (Locke, n. d.; Astri, 2017; Harris, 2012).

ARTICLE 1

Positive impact of unlimited gadget use

An advantage of gadget usage is that gadgets can reduce costs spent on books and ensure that schoolwork done is secure, thereby preventing children from falling behind at school (Levy, 2013).

Gadget usage by children can be educational and teach children a variety of functions (Harris, 2012). Besides, Internet usage by gadgets can help children learn new things (Harris, 2012). It is apparent that the right benefits need to be reaped from gadget usage, albeit when controlled (Harris, 2012).

A study by Hofferth (2010), as stated by Harris (2012), stated that test results for reading and mathematics actually improved with an increased amount of time on the computer. These support the advantage of unlimited child access to gadgets through the perceived educational value of using gadgets to teach small children new things and improve creativity (Harris, 2012; Adhikari, n. d.).

Kaufman (n. d.) stated that the decisions that parents make to allow children to use tablets are based not on verified scientific research on tablet usage, but on the consequences of passive television viewing and app developers' claims. This has resulted in significant controversy regarding usage of tablets, with some people saying they are beneficial while others suggest that the devices are harmful or don't have any clue as to their value (Kaufman, n. d.).

From the above information, it can be assumed that limiting access for children to gadgets based on parental decisions isn't necessary since they don't have adequate information to support the disadvantages (Kaufman, n. d.). Be that as it may, it is clear that there are a couple of disadvantages that should be considered.

ARTICLE 1

Negative impact on children's physical activity and security

With regards to mobile based technologies, young children love to access various mobile technological devices (Holloway, Green and Livingstone, 2013). Although there is evidence that the technological devices allow children to enjoy themselves, there is also evidence that using technological devices can negatively impact on the privacy and security of child users since the devices can track their personal information or send them links to social networking sites without warning (Holloway, Green and Livingstone, 2013).

With regard to mobile devices and internet security, there is little evidence about very young children using unique internet-enabled devices and their connections to advantages or threats related to their usage; therefore, finding and studying the usage of different devices assists them in proving the age, situation and gadgets that link better to ideal internet usage for children (Holloway, Green and Livingstone, 2013). Still, having limitations on gadget usage is essential to maintain security (Holloway, Green and Livingstone, 2013).

According to Locke (n. d.), using gadgets can lead to a reduction in physical activity, which intensifies obesity. Also, cancer causing radiation can be increased by gadget [especially mobile phone] usage (Locke, n. d.). A reduction in brain processing and effective sleeping habits caused by gadget usage also compounds the necessity for limitations (Locke, n. d.).

Invariably, it has to be noted that lack of parental control is responsible for various problems with people using gadgets, such as viewing harmful websites, excessive usage and playing inappropriate games (Rowan, 2014). While parental control is necessary, it should be more along the lines of controlling the material viewed online rather than controlling the screen time spent on gadgets (Rowan, 2014). Put simply, while the usage of gadgets needs to be controlled in time spent, the quality of content matters more in this case (Rowan, 2014).

Information acquired by students outside of school may be valuable for classroom interaction, but teachers need to be aware that it could lead to distraction and plagiarism (Ronan, 2017). Therefore, it cannot be denied that, despite privacy issues, steps have to be taken to ensure that there is no unnecessary usage of technology beyond certain limits (Ronan, 2017).

Unlimited access to gadgets can affect schoolwork negatively (Ronan, 2017). It not only negatively affects physical activity but, in the case of younger children, unlimited gadget usage can have even greater consequences for their development (Ronan, 2017; speechandlanguagekids.com, 2016).

ARTICLE 1

Negative impact on child development and family bonding

The 2017 Pediatric Academic Societies Meeting provided evidence that for every half an hour spent on handheld screens, expressive speech would be delayed by 49% of the risk of speech delay without using handheld screens (American Academy of Pediatrics, 2017).

This should be a warning for parents if they allow handheld screen usage for children below the age of two, as developing linguistic skills at this stage of their lives is crucial for their development (speechandlanguagekids.com, 2016).

Actual two-way, face-to-face conversation, which is more efficient in improving language skills compared to other ways of verbal communication, according to a study by Christakis et al (2009), as cited by Dewar (2015), is restricted when there is unlimited gadget usage by children. This contributes to delayed language skills (speechandlanguagekids.com, 2016).

For the foundations in physical, social and speech capabilities for babies, toddlers and preschool children to be developed productively, it is necessary to control the usage of gadgets in their formative years (speechandlanguagekids.com, 2016).

The usage of electronic gadgets may increase concentrations of the neurotransmitter dopamine, which is caused by stimulating fast paced swipes of the gadget used to do things (Margalit, 2016). This means that children who use gadgets more frequently are more likely to seek instant gratification and less likely to be patient with seeking results (Margalit, 2016).

Also, the frontal lobe in a child is less developed with the usage of gadgets and children become less empathetic as a result of reduced human interaction caused by the usage of gadgets (Margalit, 2016). In addition, there is the increased risk of addiction from the usage of gadgets (Margalit, 2016; Astri, 2017). Eye problems, mental problems and delayed cognitive development of crucial skills for young children are also consequences of gadget usage that impact child development [especially for young children], which is why unlimited gadget usage isn't good (Locke, n. d.).

Also, the usage of technology has reduced the time available and motivation for family bonding and traditional family activities as people tend to spend more time with their gadgets (Orlando, 2013). Actual human interaction has been reduced by online or messaged communications (Orlando, 2013).

Based on the information mentioned in the last few paragraphs, it can be stated that unlimited gadget usage worsens the future development of children (Orlando, 2013). Despite the fact that brain functions can be impacted by physical activity for several minutes, children below teenage years spend less time playing outdoors compared with time spent near a screen [including gadget usage] (League, 2015). This can cause delayed brain development as a consequence of physical activity being reduced, while exercising the brain through physical activity, through brain building and conditioning, improves people's feelings (League, 2015).

For children, it may be easy to get bored without using gadgets and parenting may be easier with an unlimited usage of gadgets by children, especially if children are addicted to gadgets (Norhidayah, 2016). However, there are many more beneficial activities that both parents and children can participate in instead of using gadgets in their free time and these tend to be more beneficial to the brain (Norhidayah, 2016; speechandlanguagekids.com, 2016; Orlando, 2013).

Reading together, playing outdoors, having family interactions and celebrating special occasions help foster family bonding (Norhidayah, 2016; speechandlanguagekids.com, 2016; Orlando, 2013). These real-world activities also bring a more realistic perception of the world to children than gadget usage regardless of the positive impacts of gadget use (Orlando, 2013).

Conclusion

Based on the research undertaken, I lean towards the opinion that children shouldn't be given unlimited access to gadgets because of the harm that they bring (Astri, 2017; Ronan, 2017; League, 2015).

Unlimited gadget access leads to problems such as addiction, privacy violations and retarded development of the brain [especially for young children] (Astri, 2017; Ronan, 2017; League, 2015).

The problems brought by unlimited access to gadgets outweigh the advantages as a whole (Astri, 2017; Ronan, 2017; League, 2015).

REFERENCES

Collected Articles

Adhikari, B. (n. d.) Advantages and disadvantages of letting your child use too much of electronic gadgets.
[Online]. Available from: https://tinyurl.com/53bkuan4
[Accessed 9 November 2017].

American Academy of Pediatrics (2017) Handheld screen time linked with speech delays in young children, eurekalert.org, 4 May.
[Online]. Available from: https://tinyurl.com/y4r99rvb
[Accessed 9 November 2017].

Astri, Y. (2017) Give attention not gadgets, New Straits Times, 31 January.
[Online]. Available from: https://tinyurl.com/3nt236en
[Accessed 9 November 2017].

Dewar, G. (2015) The effects of television on speech development: Is it helpful or harmful?
[Online]. Available from: https://tinyurl.com/2rve45bt
[Accessed 11 November 2017].

Harris, K. M. (2012) Kids can benefit from gadgets-within limits, Pocono Record, 27 July.
[Online]. Available from: https://tinyurl.com/5xr488zs
[Accessed 9 November 2017].

Holloway, D., Green, L. and Livingstone, S. (2013) Zero to Eight: Young children and their internet use.
[Online]. LSE, London: EU Kids Online, pp. 1-36. Available from: https://tinyurl.com/434hh3ex
[Accessed 7 November 2017].

Kaufman, J. (n. d.) Touch-screen Technology and Children, childmags.com.au, 24 April.
[Online]. Available from: https://tinyurl.com/yscs7hju
[Accessed 11 November 2017].

ARTICLE 1 - References

League, A. (2015) Kids and Gadgets: The Effects of Electronic Media on Developing Brains.
[Online]. Available from: https://tinyurl.com/mv58v8un
[Accessed 6 November 2017].

Levy, A. (2013) Children 'are falling behind in class' if their parents can't afford to buy them iPads and other tablet computers, dailymail.co.uk, 28 July.
[Online]. Available from: https://tinyurl.com/abttrxfx
[Accessed 9 November 2017].

Locke, R. (n. d.) 8 reasons why children should not use handheld devices frequently.
[Online]. Available from: https://tinyurl.com/2m84hxu6
[Accessed 9 November 2017].

Margalit, L. (2016) What Screen Time Can Really Do to Kids' Brains.
[Online]. Available from: https://tinyurl.com/2p469uba
[Accessed 8 November 2017].

Norhidayah, M. N. (2016) Children prefer to bond with technology than their families, New Straits Times, April 13.
[Online]. Available from: https://tinyurl.com/2fymr2r8
[Accessed 9 November 2017].

Orlando, J. (2013) Technology harming family life? Blame The Parents, The Sydney Morning Herald, 9 July.
[Online]. Available from: https://tinyurl.com/45rc5453
[Accessed 9 November 2017].

Ronan, A. (2017) The Pros and Cons of Technology.
[Online]. Available from: https://tinyurl.com/23tfh8vc
[Accessed 10 November 2017].

Collected Articles

Rowan, C. (2014) Child Sustainability - How technology addictions are killing our children, and what to do about it.
[Online]. Available from: https://tinyurl.com/huv6n86w
[Accessed 6 November 2017].

speechandlanguagekids.com (2016) Hang in there, we're going to talk about screen time...
[Online]. Available from: https://tinyurl.com/mvh77eb9
[Accessed 9 November 2017].

ARTICLE 1 - References

Collected Articles

ARTICLE 2

Pollution

Background

This article discusses pollution and its consequences (eVirtualGuru, n. d.). By definition, pollution refers to activities that dirty and harm the environment (eVirtualGuru, n. d.). Pollution is a worldwide phenomenon that affects everyone across the world and the global warming that it has caused had been discussed in the 1997 Kyoto Protocol (Vishal, n. d.). However, this problem has yet to be solved effectively (Vishal, n. d.).

Pollution can be caused by the release of waste, chemicals and other environmentally damaging agents into anywhere in the environment (Rinkesh, n. d.). There are many types of pollution worldwide, consisting of land, air and water pollution based on the locations affected, and all these forms of pollution result in the addition of harmful substances into the environment (eVirtualGuru, n. d.). The Latin word 'pollution', which means to make dirty, is the basis for the word 'pollution' as used in this article (eVirtualGuru, n. d.).

Problem Statement

Environmental pollution, which is known as the alteration of our surroundings until the changes produced become unfavourable to the environment, is the result of environmental changes induced by human activities (eVirtualGuru, n. d.). Activities responsible for such changes are deforestation, waste disposal, industrial processes, the excessive usage of motor vehicles, open burnings and increased gasoline and nuclear energy usage (Curiosity Aroused, 2013), resulting in global warming (Becker, 2017). Global warming refers to the increase in the average global temperature and has resulted in melting ice and worldwide flooding, differences in worldwide sea levels and the decreasing numbers of several species (Becker, 2017; Rinkesh, n. d.).

Another form of pollution is soil pollution, which is caused by dumping solid, semi-solid and liquid wastes into the soil along with household chemical products, atmospheric fallout, nuclear fallout and the disposal of nuclear waste (Agarwal and Sangal, 2008). The hazardous materials consequently pollute the soil and make it unsuitable for agriculture (Agarwal and Sangal, 2008), thereby creating health problems in humans (Kennedy, 2017). It is a problem that needs to be tackled urgently (Agarwal and Sangal, 2008).

Research Objective

(See Research Questions below)

What are the reasons for pollution today?

The major reasons for pollution, as listed earlier, are excessive motor vehicle [especially car] usage, industrial processes, open burnings, emissions of greenhouse gases from the combustion of fuels, usage of gasoline and nuclear energy usage (Curiosity Aroused, 2013).

How does pollution affect the environment?

Pollution affects the environment through global warming from the trapping of heat by the increased release of carbon dioxide, resulting in the extinction of several species and the disruption of the balance of nature and even the inhalation of several greenhouse gases like carbon monoxide (United States Green Building Council, n. d.; Rinkesh, n. d.; Curiosity Aroused, 2013).

Limitations of study

To research about global warming, land pollution, soil pollution and their effects.

Significance of the Study

To bring awareness about global warming, land pollution, soil pollution and their effects to the public.

Methodology

Use internet articles.

Introduction

As stated in the previous page, pollution refers to irresponsible activities that harm the environment (eVirtualGuru, n. d.).

Pollution is a severe and worldwide phenomenon that impacts the wellness of everybody's quality of life through carbon dioxide emissions, extinction of species and inhalation of greenhouse gases (United States Green Building Council, n. d.; Rinkesh, n. d.; Curiosity Aroused, 2013). The paragraphs below aim to address this issue.

The main pollution issue is environmental pollution, which, as stated above, is the alteration of our surroundings until the changes produced become unfavourable to the environment (eVirtualGuru, n. d.). The main types of environmental pollution and their consequences to be discussed below are global warming, land pollution and soil pollution and their respective consequences (United States Environmental Protection Agency, 2017; Rinkesh, n. d.).

Main Theme 1

Pollution and its effects - examples of pollution-causing activities and the effects of pollution.

There are several examples of activities that can cause pollution (Curiosity Aroused, 2013). For example, open burning of various harmful items into the atmosphere, greenhouse gas emissions by car usage and the combustion of fossil fuels are activities that are polluting because they cause damage to the environment (Curiosity Aroused, 2013).

Similarly, deforestation and chemical overuse for agriculture can also be considered as pollution because of the damage inflicted on the environment through habitat destruction, soil contamination and the loss of trees (Environmental Defense Fund, 2017; Rinkesh, n. d.).

There is evidence that deforestation has a worse impact on the environment compared to the massive usage of cars and trucks on the road (Earth Talk, 2012). The World Carfree Network (WCN) stated that motor vehicles hold the responsibility for approximately 14 percent of global fossil fuel burning-caused carbon dioxide emissions, while most analysts believed deforestation was responsible for 15 percent (World Carfree Network, 2009; Earth Talk, 2012).

The Environmental Defense Fund (EDF), a leading green group, stated that, annually from 2000 to 2009, tropical rainforests lost 32 million acres to chopping and burning—and deforestation is only increasing as time passes (Environmental Defense Fund, 2017). According to the EDF, deforestation will result in carbon being released into the atmosphere to the equivalent of another 200 billion tons in years to come unless the system that now encourages deforestation is amended (Environmental Defense Fund, 2017).

Sub Theme 1

Polluting mechanisms' contributions to global warming.

Mechanisms that contribute to pollution in general also contribute to global warming (Curiosity Aroused, 2013). For example, motor vehicles [especially cars] that emit chemicals and gases like lead and nitrogen oxide [besides the inhaled carbon monoxide] also increase carbon dioxide emissions that trap heat in the atmosphere, besides methane and hydrofluorocarbon emissions that have a higher potential to cause global warming than carbon dioxide (Curiosity Aroused, 2013; eVirtualGuru, n. d.; United States Environmental Protection Agency, 2017).

Another large contributor to global warming is the construction industry as construction has led to emissions of carbon dioxide through electricity consumption (United States Green Building Council, n. d.). In a study conducted in 2004, it was found that about 39% of the United States' total carbon dioxide emissions were caused by emissions from buildings (United States Green Building Council, n. d.).

Sub Theme 2

Effects of global warming that prove global warming is a form of pollution and a result of polluting activities.

As a result of global warming, sea ice around the world has melted and since polar bears need the ice to survive and hunt for prey, the melting of ice has resulted in their decreasing numbers (Fears, 2017). Also, when combined with deforestation, this has resulted in an increase of floods due to rising sea levels from increased melting of ice, besides disrupting the ecosystem due to soil pollution and the destruction of habitats for animals to live in (Earth Talk, 2012; Becker, 2017; Rinkesh, n. d.).

Potential heat-related deaths, according to researchers from Brown University, are among the likely consequences of global warming in the future (Blumer, 2017). Increased allergies from global warming may also point to pollution caused by global warming through increased exposure to allergens caused by global warming (Barnes, PHD, et al, 2013).

As global warming is caused by carbon dioxide emissions that trap heat in the atmosphere with nitrous oxide and a variety of greenhouse gases, polluting motor vehicles and the construction industry that causes pollution with carbon dioxide, there is evidence that global warming is not just a form of pollution by itself alone, but also a result of pollution (United States Environmental Protection Agency, 2017; Curiosity Aroused, 2013; United States Green Building Council, n. d.).

Main Theme 2

Land Pollution.

Land pollution refers to activities that harm the earth's surface [including its soil] (Rinkesh, n. d.). For example, deforestation is a form of land pollution through the cutting down of trees that absorb carbon dioxide, resulting in global warming, with carbon being released from cut trees into the environment (Earth Talk, 2012). Such pollution can be termed as the deterioration in quality of initially fertile land that could be used constructively for other purposes, but with the initially fertile land being harmed by degradation (Rinkesh, n. d.).

In the name of development, anthropogenic activities are committed (Rinkesh, n. d.). Land is severely affected by such activities (Rinkesh, n. d.). In other words, there is a drastic reduction in land quality and/or productivity, resulting in a negative impact on agriculture, forestation, construction and so on (Rinkesh, n. d.).

There is a general tendency to view water and air pollution more seriously because of the more visible effects of these forms of pollution, and the damage inflicted on the environment through land pollution is ignored until phenomena such as global warming occur (Rinkesh, n. d.). Therefore, land pollution needs to be considered as serious a form of pollution as water and air pollution, especially for the future of the planet (Rinkesh, n. d.).

Sub Theme 1

Soil Pollution

Soil pollution is pollution that affects the soil by damaging it, especially the soil's upper level (Rinkesh, n. d.). This form of pollution is caused by chemical fertilisers and pesticides being used excessively in the soil (Rinkesh, n. d.). Harmful substances released by other forms of pollution such as acid rain, radioactive fallout, fuel leakage and unhealthy waste management also contribute to soil contamination (Everything Connects, 2014). Another point to note is that, while chemicals such as lead and mercury can be natural, they are harmful in high amounts or foreign to the soil, and adding them into the soil will worsen the effects of soil pollution (Everything Connects, 2014).

Soil pollution also affects the food chain through worsening microorganisms' and arthropods' metabolism (Everything Connects, 2014). Increased cancer rates can occur through carcinogenic agents which can be assimilated by humans through the consumption of polluted food (Everything Connects, 2014). Brain damage (if food is polluted by metals) has been known to be a tragic outcome (Everything Connects, 2014). Although the soil may naturally contain lead and mercury, high concentrations of either metal due to soil pollution by either metal can interfere with children's brain development and lead to subsequent neurological problems (Everything Connects, 2014; Etherington, 2011). Exposure to excessive mercury in soil can also cause kidney and liver damage (Everything Connects, 2014).

With volatile compounds released by soil pollution into the atmosphere, such pollution becomes a contributor to air pollution, and when toxic compounds and toxic chemicals with dangerous heavy metals from soil pollution leach into groundwater or contaminate runoff or sewage before polluting water sources through reaching streams, lakes or oceans, water pollution invariably worsens (Everything Connects, 2014).

Sub Theme 2

Effects of Land pollution on the entire world.

Land pollution is responsible for the loss of habitats for animals to live in (Rinkesh, n. d.). The displacement of animals will reduce their numbers, putting them at risk of becoming extinct since it will be harder for them to adapt to their new circumstances (Rinkesh, n. d.).

Deforestation and soil erosion result in fertile land turning dry or barren (Rinkesh, n. d.). Once this happens, the land can never be fertile again, regardless of the quantities and quality of measures to redeem its fertility (Rinkesh, n. d.). Land conversion, involving altering land use for specific purposes, is another major cause of land pollution as it seriously disrupts the land's previous use immensely (Rinkesh, n. d.).

Also, land is constantly wasted as available land turns unproductive without years of utilization; the affected land then becomes useless (Rinkesh, n. d.). Potent land is tampered with to acquire extra land, affecting its indigenous state (Rinkesh, n. d.). Toxic chemicals and pesticides present in contaminated land cause diseases of the human respiratory system and skin cancer (Rinkesh, n. d.). The toxic chemicals can reach our bodies and animals through fruit and vegetables grown in polluted soil that we and animals eat (Rinkesh, n. d.). Biomagnification, which harms ecology severely, occurs when the toxic chemicals are ingested by the animals of the ecosystem through fruits and vegetables in contact with soil contaminated by the chemicals (Rinkesh, n. d.).

Finally, disruption of the ecosystem balance and habitat destruction due to land pollution can cause global warming through deforestation when combined with air and water pollution, the greenhouse effect and open burnings, which leads to consequences such as unusual weather patterns and flash floods (Rinkesh, n. d.).

Conclusion

To conclude, the consequences of pollution are the release of carbon dioxide, the ingestion of toxic chemicals, an increase of floods, global warming and the destruction of habitats for animals to live in (United States Green Building Council, n. d.; Rinkesh, n. d.; Becker, 2017; Blumer, 2017).

REFERENCES

Collected Articles

Agarwal, R. K. and Sangal, V. K. (2008) Environmental Pollution, In: Krishna's Environment and Ecology, Goel, Dr. N. (eds.), Meerut: Krishna House, 11, Shivaji Road, pp. 117-119.
[Online]. Available from: Google Books. https://tinyurl.com/5erp4apc
[Accessed 19 October 2017].

Barnes, C. S., PHD, Alexis, N. E., Bernstein, J.A., Cohn, J.R., Demain, J. G., Horner, E., Levetin, E., Nel, A., and Phipatanakul, W. (2013) Climate Change and Our Environment: The Effect on Respiratory and Allergic Disease, J Allergy Clin Immunol Pract, March, 1 (2), pp. 137–141.
[Online]. Available from: https://tinyurl.com/2psd26zr
[Accessed 18 October 2017].

Becker, R. (2017) A future of more extreme floods, brought to you by climate change.
[Online]. Available from: https://tinyurl.com/48k2bmkj
[Accessed 18 October 2017].

Blumer, A. (2017) Climate Change Could Cause Heat-Related Deaths to Spike for 10 Major U.S. Cities, Study Says.
[Online]. Available from: https://tinyurl.com/yn9cdfwd
[Accessed 18 October 2017].

Curiosity Aroused (2013) The 10 Worst Modern Causes of Air Pollution.
[Online]. Available from: https://tinyurl.com/yjktemz7
[Accessed 15 October 2017].

Earth Talk (2012) Deforestation and Its Extreme Effect on Global Warming.
[Online]. Available from: https://tinyurl.com/um3hw9bp
[Accessed 14 October 2017].

Environmental Defense Fund (2017) REDD+: Protecting tropical forests.
[Online]. Available from: https://tinyurl.com/y7ak2tj5
[Accessed 14 October 2017].

ARTICLE 2 - References

Etherington, K. (2011) Philadelphia EPA Public Hearing Testimony.
[Online]. Available from: https://tinyurl.com/weyk4jd8
[Accessed 14 October 2017].

Everything Connects (2014) Soil Pollution.
[Online]. Available from: https://tinyurl.com/2yr9mrzn
[Accessed 14 October 2017].

eVirtualGuru (n. d.) Essay on "Pollution" Complete Essay for Class 10, Class 12 and Graduation and other classes.
[Online]. Available from: https://tinyurl.com/yc3we9kw
[Accessed 15 October 2017].

Fears, D. (2017) Without action on climate change, say goodbye to polar bears.
[Online]. Available from: https://tinyurl.com/34y7vtur
[Accessed 15 October 2017].

Kennedy, A. L. (2017) The Effects of Soil Pollution on Humans.
[Online]. Available from: https://tinyurl.com/duzae8hm
[Accessed 14 October 2017].

Rinkesh (n. d.) What is Land Pollution?
[Online]. Available from: https://tinyurl.com/47xpkvxb
[Accessed 14 October 2017].

Pollution Issues (2017) Soil Pollution.
[Online]. Available from: https://tinyurl.com/2886pm4e
[Accessed 14 October 2017].

United States Environmental Protection Agency (2017) Greenhouse Gas Emissions from a Typical Passenger Vehicle.
[Online]. Available from: https://tinyurl.com/thn7rtc7
[Accessed 15 October 2017].

Collected Articles

Vishal (n. d.) 1309 Words Essay on Global Warming: Causes, Effects and Remedies.
[Online]. Available from: https://tinyurl.com/3vdxcj5h
[Accessed 19 October 2017].

World Carfree Network (2009) Some Statistics.
[Online]. Available from: https://tinyurl.com/z5df7w55
[Accessed 14 October 2017].

ARTICLE 2 - References

Collected Articles

ARTICLE 3

Fella Design's success in branding

1.0 Introduction

The topic selected discusses what makes Fella Design successful in branding based on the presentation given by Mr. Andrew Chen (FEM Mediahaus, 2020). In the presentation, Mr. Andrew Chen stated how Fella Design, his company, went from being an ordinary furniture store to becoming a successful chain store selling furniture under his management (FEM Mediahaus, 2020).

Fella Design, also known as Fella Design Sdn Bhd, is a store that specialises in selling furniture such as sofas for homes (Selva, 2016; FEM Mediahaus, 2020). The presentation delivered by Mr. Andrew Chen discussed how the usage of brand elements played a major role in Fella Design's success with branding (FEM Mediahaus, 2020).

In addition, what goes behind Fella Design's branding, challenges, competition, marketing strategies and recommendations in strategies to Fella Design will also be discussed in the assignment (Keller and Swaminathan, 2020; Fella Design, 2020b; Fella Design, 2018b; Palmatier and Sridhar, 2017; Zaman, 2018).

2.0 Elements

By definition, a brand distinguishes the goods or services of a group of sellers or a seller from those produced by their competitors (Keller and Swaminathan, 2020). There are various elements which create a brand, such as brand name, symbol, term, sign and design (Keller and Swaminathan, 2020).

An element of Fella Design's brand is brand name (Keller and Swaminathan, 2020). According to the presentation by Andrew Chen, brand name and branding have been emphasized by Fella Design in order to identify and differentiate Fella Design's products and services from those of its competitors with an emphasis by Fella Design on the unique and standard design used by the company to design the company's furniture with elegance and customization to suit its customers (Keller and Swaminathan, 2020; FEM Mediahaus, 2020).

The usage of the brand name by Fella Design can be defined by naming guidelines which show that Fella Design's products are intended to be customer–friendly (Fella Design using the word 'fella' for its brand and to identify its products) and identifiable with Fella Design in quality and production (Keller and Swaminathan, 2020; Puspadevi, 2012).

Fella Design does not have a brand symbol but a brand logo. By definition, a brand symbol is descriptive while a logo does not use a script to describe the brand (Fella Design, 2020b; Keller and Swaminathan, 2020). The brand logo element of Fella Design has been developed to help establish the company as a manufacturer of quality products and to increase the purchase of their products (Keller and Swaminathan, 2020; Gyambrah and Sherry, 2017). The logo is used in advertisements promoting the high quality of the furniture sold by Fella Design with the aim of increasing the company's customer base (Fella Design, 2020b).

Brand logo of Fella Design (Fella Design, 2020a)

In addition, URLs have been used as another brand element to define Fella Design with Fella Design's website (Alnsour and Subbah, 2018). This is through URLs defining the locations of web pages online (Alnsour and Subbah, 2018). The URL of Fella Design (https://fella.com.my/) has been selected as it is a unique URL without previous usage and with the ability to define Fella Design as a different company from other companies (Fella Design, 2018a; Keller and Swaminathan, 2020).

Despite the potential danger of cybersquatting or abuse of Fella Design's URL, Fella Design's URL is secure for the moment, eliminating the need for measures to be taken by Fella Design to secure its URL at this moment (Keller and Swaminathan, 2020; Fella Design, 2018a). This security should allow Fella Design to focus its efforts on furniture production and sales (Fella Design, 2020b).

Despite a lack of packaging usage, Fella Design has made brand design a priority (Keller and Swaminathan, 2020). However, with regard to other brand elements, it must be noted that Fella Design has not used brand signs or brand characters for branding purposes (Keller and Swaminathan, 2020).

In any event, given Fella Design's prioritization on selling furniture, brand characters with human or real-life characteristics to represent the products and advertisements of Fella Design are unnecessary (Fella Design, 2020b; Keller and Swaminathan, 2020). Similarly, brand sign and brand term are brand elements not used by Fella Design due to a lack of necessity (Fella Design, 2020b; Keller and Swaminathan, 2020).

3.0 What goes behind the brand

With regard to the brand name element emphasized by Fella Design, the usage of the brand name by Fella Design can be defined by naming guidelines to show that Fella Design's products are intended to be customer–friendly (with Fella Design using the word fella, meaning 'friend', for identifying its brand and its products according to Puspadevi (2012) and identifiable with Fella Design in quality and production (Keller and Swaminathan, 2020; FEM Mediahaus, 2020). This is an application of brand associations in the form of associating and reinforcing Fella Design's reputation with friendliness, familiarity and meaningfulness to its customers (Keller and Swaminathan, 2020). Such brand associations, when applied to Fella Design, can not only attract customers but also create a sense of familiarity with Fella Design (Keller and Swaminathan, 2020).

Another aspect of branding emphasized by Fella Design with its usage of 'Fella' in its brand name is brand distinctiveness in a desirable manner through using the word 'Fella', which means "friend" (FEM Mediahaus, 2020; Keller and Swaminathan, 2020; Puspadevi, 2012). This is in addition to the brand awareness which can be generated by the Fella Design brand name being easy to pronounce, distinctive and familiar (Keller and Swaminathan, 2020). Such factors help enhance the Fella Design brand name

(Keller and Swaminathan, 2020). Word-of-mouth also helps raise its awareness among buyers (Keller and Swaminathan, 2020). Finally, the usage of the word 'Fella' also suggests specific information about Fella Design's brand (Keller and Swaminathan, 2020; Puspadevi, 2012).

To promote its branding, Fella Design has participated in branding events such as the Malaysian International Furniture Fair (MIFF, 2015). This was to promote the quality and completion of Fella Design's products while reducing the explanations needed to promote Fella Design in branding (MIFF, 2015).

In fact, Manivanan Madhavan, Fella Design's 2015 Chief Operating Officer, stated that the branding of Fella Design's products at the Malaysian International Furniture Fair could be interpreted as better than branding as done by other companies as it showed that Fella Design was better prepared to produce and exhibit high quality products than its competitors (MIFF, 2015). The company also used the MIFF to raise its profile among participating foreigners and improve its brand's reputation overseas (MIFF, 2015).

4.0 Challenges

Throughout its history, Fella Design has encountered various challenges (EverydayOnSales, 2019). An example of a challenge experienced by Fella Design was the challenge of competing with furniture stores in producing the best furniture which could be displayed and gaining more sales and stores compared to other furniture stores (Wong, 2016; Fella Design, 2020b).

In addition, it faced the challenge of recession during its foundation in the mid 1980's and the 1990's Financial Crisis in Malaysia, which caused Fella Design to restructure its branding and cancel its plans for overseas stores due to a lack of funding (EverydayOnSales, 2019; Samphantharak, 2019; Kam, 2008).

Other challenges faced by Fella Design included the company's loss of millions of Ringgit Malaysia in a financial crisis, cash flow management and exploitation of expansion plans (Kam, 2008).

Despite these challenges, the management of Fella Design, with careful strategic planning, has helped the company survive the financial crisis, albeit with setbacks such as closed overseas stores (Kam, 2008).

5.0 Competition

Fella Design encountered competition from several furniture stores, both locally and internationally, in Indonesia, Thailand, China and Vietnam, thereby threatening its prospects (The New Straits Times Press, 2019; Ratnasingam, 2017). Fortunately, it was able to perform well enough against its local competitors to have the means to maintain several overseas stores in addition to 250 Malaysian (including 21 physical) stores as already mentioned in Andrew Chen's presentation (The New Straits Times Press, 2019; Fella Design, 2018b).

Fella Design's competitors include Lorenzo, IKEA and Lamex Decor (Tiendeo, 2020a). Nevertheless, it has more stores in Malaysia than these companies (Fella Design, 2018b; IKEA Malaysia, 2020; Tiendeo, 2020b; Lorenzo International Limited, 2019).

According to Andrew Chen, Fella Design successfully increased its annual product sales between 1985 and 2015 amidst competition, with a peak of 100,000,000 products sold annually in 2005, and, despite a significant decrease to 65,000,000 products sold annually in 2015, Fella Design managed to increase the number of products it sold annually between 2015 and 2020.

6.0 Marketing Strategies

By definition, a marketing strategy refers to a course of actions and decisions undertaken by a company to produce a unique and sustainable advantage over its competitors while producing value for its customers (Palmatier and Sridhar, 2017). For Fella Design to succeed with sustainably successful marketing strategies, it needs to select several marketing strategies which provide profits and value to its customers (Palmatier and Sridhar, 2017).

In addition, marketing strategy sustainability and company success need to be seen from the customer perspective and the impact on a company's brand equity based on the company's choice of marketing strategy is another concern which should define the company's marketing strategy choice (Palmatier and Sridhar, 2017; Keller and Swaminathan, 2020). Examples of marketing strategies are product, price, place and promotion strategies, strategies based on the 4p's (product, price, place and promotion) of marketing (Keller and Swaminathan, 2020; David and David, 2017).

An example of a marketing strategy which has been followed by Fella Design is the price strategy, given that Fella Design has reduced prices for its furniture products to attract customers to its special 2019 year-end sales with cheaper but still decent quality furniture (Fella Design, 2020b). Setting lower prices for products is an aspect of value pricing, which uses the most suitable combination of product costs, product prices and product quality (Keller and Swaminathan, 2020). In Fella Design's 2019 year-end sales, value pricing has been used to get customers to buy furniture with high perceived product quality and suitably low product prices so as to improve the company's 2019 sales at the end of 2019 without being constrained by a fixed price strategy (Fella Design, 2020b; Barros and Sousa, 2019).

In addition, prices have been set by Fella Design for its products to reflect the brand's value and the products' value and customer–perceived value, or how much Fella Design's customers are willing to pay to obtain the products (Keller and Swaminathan, 2020; Fella Design, 2020b). That said, there are discounts set for the same products by Fella Design to increase sales during promotional events (Fella Design, 2020b). This is another example of the price strategy being utilized by Fella Design with customer–perceived value determining the actual marketplace prices for its products (Keller and Swaminathan, 2020; Fella Design, 2020b).

Fella Design's product strategy is based on the principle of customer–perceived quality, that is, customers see its products as being of a higher quality than those of similar products sold by its competitors. (Fella Design, 2020b; Keller and Swaminathan, 2020). This is to generate positive attitudes from customers to the Fella Design brand, resulting in increased sales and usage of Fella

Design's products (Keller and Swaminathan, 2020). Another aspect of product strategy used by Fella Design is good customer service by, for example, allowing customers to trade used sofas for newer sofas (Keller and Swaminathan, 2020; Fella Design, 2018c).

The place strategy Fella Design uses is through its strategic selection of urban streets and malls as places to launch its stores (David and David, 2017; Fella Design, 2018b). This can explain why Fella Design has 22 Malaysian physical stores in operation as of 2020 and had 21 operational physical stores in Malaysia in 2018 (Fella Design, 2018b). Also, with regard to sales territories, Fella Design has chosen to prioritize sales in Malaysia as the company has higher chances of success with Malaysian sales than overseas sales (David and David, 2017; Fella Design, 2018b; Kam, 2008).

Finally, the promotion strategy, in the form of advertising and sales promotion, is an important aspect of Fella Design's operation (Fella Design, 2020b; David and David, 2017). This can be seen in Fella Design's 2019 year-end sales promotion, in which the statements "best deals ever" and "last sale of the year" were used to encourage purchases of Fella Design's products through purchase incentives in December 2019 (Ya-Ping, 2017; Fella Design, 2020b).

For several other sales promotions, Fella Design used price discounts (Fella Design, 2020b; Ya-Ping, 2017). Another promotion variable as used by Fella Design involved the use of advertisements about the features/characteristics of Fella Design's products by the company itself (David and David, 2017; Fella Design, 2020b).

7.0 Recommendations

A recommendation strategy which can be made to Fella Design is to produce furniture which works well and is of improved quality compared to earlier furniture while providing a satisfactory customer–perceived value to the company's customers (Zaman, 2018; Keller and Swaminathan, 2020). The marketing strategy and branding efforts to be used by Fella Design after producing such furniture in branding can be based on others' suggestions if appropriate, but still need to reflect and maintain a sustainable competitive advantage over the branding efforts of its competitors, both in the marketing strategy and the marketed products (Hasnah et al, 2010; Palmatier and Sridhar, 2017). It will help if Fella Design looks at the characteristics which define good products such as quality, brand name, service level and features and options before designing and selling its improved quality furniture for this recommendation strategy (David and David, 2017; Fella Design, 2020b).

In addition, to support the aforementioned recommendation strategy, a good promotional strategy with the usage of advertising, sales promotion and personal selling is ideal (David and David, 2017). Within this recommendation strategy, the role of the price element in price level, discounts and allowances should be evaluated carefully as it is also crucial to Fella Design's success within this strategy, especially in encouraging sales during sales promotional events (David and David, 2017; Fella Design, 2020b). Finally, it is best if the improved quality furniture is sold in strategically located shops in streets and malls as a usage of the place element in outlet locations, sales territories and distribution channels (David and David, 2017; Fella Design, 2020b).

Another recommendation strategy for Fella Design's marketing strategy is to re-enter foreign markets and market products with appropriate promotional strategies to increase sales there (Kam, 2008; Daniel, 2018). It would benefit Fella Design if it could learn from its past mistakes in overseas markets in order to sustain its presence without repeating these mistakes in overseas markets (Kam, 2008).

When branding and promoting furniture overseas with this strategy, it is essential that Fella Design studies the needs of its overseas markets and provides appropriate furniture to these markets' needs and segments (Keller and Swaminathan, 2020; David and David, 2017). For this strategy to work, it is important to select suitable outlet locations, distribution channels and sales territories in overseas markets (David and David, 2017; Cuellar-Healey, 2013). Product and price elements, too, need to be considered carefully in order to achieve sustainable success in overseas markets (David and David, 2017).

The last recommendation strategy which has been suggested to Fella Design for its operations is to improve customization of its existing local products to cater for more diverse market segment needs (David and David, 2017). This is because, despite its success in customizing foreign–inspired furniture to the needs of local customers, Fella Design needs to put more effort into market segmentation for its promotional events based on geographic, demographic, psychographic and behavioural elements such as customer age, gender, usage rate and benefits sought (Fella Design, 2020b; David and David, 2017).

This can increase the likelihood of customer satisfaction and the customers being targeted with furniture and sales promotions that satisfy their needs and wants (David and David, 2017). It is expected that such a strategy will also result in higher customer retention rates since Fella Design will be selling furniture with attributes closer to the new customers' needs and attributes compared to those of older customers' needs and attributes (David and David, 2017).

8.0 Conclusion

In conclusion, it can be stated that Fella Design has succeeded in distinguishing itself from its competitors and creating its own identity with its branding efforts (FEM Mediahaus, 2020). With regard to choosing a suitable brand name, Fella Design can be considered as successful because its brand name evokes a sense of customer–friendliness (Puspadevi, 2012). Fella Design has also used its brand logo to identify its products in anticipation of promotional sales in advertising (Keller and Swaminathan, 2020; Fella Design, 2020b). To enhance the branding of Fella Design, the company used the word "Fella" for its brand name (Puspadevi, 2012). In addition, the company also took part in exhibitions such as the Malaysian International Furniture Fair (MIFF, 2015). Despite challenges faced by Fella Design from overseas competition and even locally, it was able to succeed in Malaysia (The New Straits Times Press, 2019; Fella Design, 2018b).

With regard to the marketing mix, it must be noted that Fella Design has utilised all the 4p's of the marketing mix in creating its strategies (Keller and Swaminathan, 2020; David and David, 2017). It has been recommended that Fella Design adopt a strategy which enables it to produce better quality furniture than before while allowing the company to provide satisfactory customer–perceived value to its customers buying its products (Zaman,

2018; Keller and Swaminathan, 2020). Another recommendation strategy which can be adopted by Fella Design is allowing the company to maintain a competitive advantage and a sustained presence over its competitors in overseas operations (The New Straits Times Press, 2019; Kam, 2008). By using all the 4 p's, Fella Design will be in a strong position to ensure these strategies' success (David and David, 2017). Finally, Fella Design can also adopt a strategy for Fella Design's products to be customized more precisely to the needs of various market segments as a recommendation strategy (David and David, 2017).

REFERENCES

Collected Articles

Alnsour, M. S. and Subbah, M. L. (2018) Impact of brand elements on brand equity: An applied study on Jordanian Corporations, African Journal of Marketing Management, March, 10 (3), pp. 17–27.
[Online]. Available from: https://tinyurl.com/2frwttjr
[Accessed 27 February 2020].

Barros, C. L. and Sousa, B. (2019) Price and Marketing Strategy in Tourism Contexts: A preliminary study to mitigating seasonality, International Journal of Marketing, Communication and New Media, June, 7 (12), pp. 24–38.
[Online]. Available from: https://tinyurl.com/5h8f9845
[Accessed 23 February 2020].

Cuellar-Healey, S. (2013) Placement: Key Factors in Choosing a Distribution Channel, pp. 1–3.
[Online]. Available from: https://tinyurl.com/4wrsfzc4
[Accessed 24 February 2020].

Daniel, C. O. (2018) Effects Of Marketing Strategies On Organizational Performance, International Journal of Business Marketing and Management, September, 3 (9), pp. 1–9.
[Online]. Available from: https://tinyurl.com/yzk56dsx
[Accessed 24 February 2020].

David, F. R. and David, F. R. (2017) Strategic Management: A Competitive Advantage Approach, Concepts and Cases. 16th Edition. Harlow: Pearson Education Limited, pp. 289-292.

EverydayOnSales (2019) The biggest Most Home Furniture Warehouse Sale of Fella Design.
[Online]. Available from: https://tinyurl.com/3zxa8jjs
[Accessed 21 February 2020].

Fella Design (2018a) Fella Design.
[Online]. Available from: https://fella.com.my/
[Accessed 22 February 2020].

ARTICLE 3 - References

Fella Design (2018b) Location.
[Online]. Available from: https://fella.com.my/location
[Accessed 23 February 2020].

Fella Design (2018c) Trade-In Your Old Sofa.
[Online]. Available from: https://fella.com.my/trade-in
[Accessed 24 February 2020].

Fella Design (2020a) Fella Design.
[Online]. Available from: https://www.facebook.com/FellaDesign/
[Accessed 28 February 2020].

Fella Design (2020b) Fella Design Juru Warehouse.
[Online]. Available from: https://www.facebook.com/felladesignjuru/
[Accessed 21 February 2020].

FEM Mediahaus (2020) Fella Design Sdn Bhd.
[Online]. Available from: https://tinyurl.com/rdejshyn
[Accessed 21 February 2020].

Gyambrah, M. and Sherry, Y. H. (2017) The role of logos in brand personality of organizations, African Journal of Business Management, July, 11 (14), pp. 327-336.
[Online]. Available from: https://tinyurl.com/ydfurwrz
[Accessed 26 February 2020].

Hasnah, H., Ishak, I., Sofri, Y., Siti, N. A. K. and Ganesan, Y. (2010) Case of Successful Malaysian Small And Medium Enterprises (SMEs): Does Business Advisory Services Help? Universiti Sains Malaysia, pp. 1-126.
[Online]. Available from: https://tinyurl.com/yc6abczw
[Accessed 24 February 2020].

IKEA Malaysia (2020) Visit your local store.
[Online]. Available from: https://www.ikea.com/my/en/stores/
[Accessed 25 February 2020].

Collected Articles

Kam, R. (2008) Taking Challenges In Its Stride.
[Online]. Available from: https://tinyurl.com/vr8dcjzr
[Accessed 24 February 2020].

Keller, K. L. and Swaminathan, V. (2020) Strategic Brand Management Building, Measuring, and Managing Brand Equity, 5th Edition, Harlow: Pearson Education Limited, pp. 32-205.

Lorenzo International Limited (2019) Locate Us.
[Online]. Available from: https://www.lorenzo-international.com/
[Accessed 25 February 2020].

MIFF (2015) Furnish Now.
[Online]. Available from: https://tinyurl.com/3h8bzmc4
[Accessed 21 February 2020].

Palmatier, R. W. and Sridhar, S. (2017) Marketing Strategy: Based on First Principles and Data Analytics, London: Palgrave, pp. 4–5.
[Online]. Available from: Google Books. https://tinyurl.com/3ekb2v5a
[Accessed 23 February 2020].

Puspadevi, S. (2012) Winning designs After almost 30 years, home-grown brand Fella Holdings Bhd is still going strong in the furnishing industry.
[Online]. Available from: https://tinyurl.com/yc6xz88t
[Accessed 23 February 2020].

Ratnasingam, J. (2017) The Malaysian Furniture Industry Charting Its Growth Potential, Universiti Putra Malaysia: Inaugural Lecture, pp. 1–108.
[Online]. Available from: https://tinyurl.com/y7y6pscb
[Accessed 21 February 2020].

Samphantharak, K. (2019) Economic Crises in Southeast Asia, February, San Diego: University of California, pp. 1–52.
[Online]. Available from: https://tinyurl.com/yckdh63r
[Accessed 21 February 2020].

ARTICLE 3 - References

Selva, M. T. (2016) Milestone for furniture retailer. *[Online]. Available from: https://tinyurl.com/ycyxjapm [Accessed 20 February 2020].*

The New Straits Times Press (2019) Fella eyes Thai, Indonesian markets. *[Online]. Available from: https://tinyurl.com/jwub2ekm [Accessed 21 February 2020].*

Tiendeo (2020a) Fella Design Catalogue, Sales & Promotions 2020. *[Online]. Available from: https://tinyurl.com/6xevuc3f [Accessed 22 February 2020].*

Tiendeo (2020b) Lamex Décor Catalogue, Sales & Promotions 2020. *[Online]. Available from: https://tinyurl.com/58tveaer [Accessed 25 February 2020].*

Wong, L. Z. (2016) Bright future for Malaysian furniture. *[Online]. Available from: https://tinyurl.com/ca8m64jk [Accessed 21 February 2020].*

Ya-Ping, A. C. (2017) A Study on the Effects of Sales Promotion on Consumer Involvement and Purchase Intention in Tourism Industry, Eurasia Journal of Mathematics, Science and Technology Education, 13 (12), pp. 8323–8330. *[Online]. Available from: https://tinyurl.com/nhbhk664 [Accessed 24 February 2020].*

Zaman, A. K. M. N. (2018) Internship Report On Daraz 'A deep dive into the branding strategies of Daraz Bangladesh Ltd', Dhaka: BRAC University, pp. 1-44. *[Online]. Available from: https://tinyurl.com/3vatwsy8 [Accessed 24 February 2020].*

Collected Articles

ARTICLE 4

Doctrine of Frustration

Introduction

The doctrine by frustration is a doctrine used to terminate contracts using means of discharge by frustration (LawTeacher, 2013e). It is a mean to discharge contracts, the others being discharge by performance and discharge by breach (Lee and Detta, 2014).

When a party has pledged to carry out a contract, the contract has to be carried out under the doctrine of absolute liability, unless specific circumstances require a discharge of contract (Lee and Detta, 2014). As to how the doctrine by frustration and its usage as a discharge can occur, the circumstances needed for a successful discharge by frustration will be discussed (LawTeacher, 2013e; Birmingham, 1989; Lee and Detta, 2014).

ARTICLE 4

How discharge by frustration can occur

Discharge by frustration can occur due to an unforeseen event which makes a contract impossible to be fulfilled to the contract's original conditions or its parties' original intentions, provided that the event occurred as a result of an external event outside the parties' control (Lawteacher, 2013e; Birmingham, 1989).

Section 57 (2) of the Contracts Act 1950 states that a contract is frustrated if it involves doing something illegal or impossible after the contract has been signed (Lee and Detta, 2014). Under the doctrine by frustration, liabilities to a contractual agreement due to failure to fulfil a contractual agreement's requirements are no longer binding if one or more parties to the agreement cannot meet the requirements because of events which cannot be controlled by the affected party or parties (LawTeacher, 2013d).

In these situations, compelling contractual performance may be unfair to the injured party according to the law (LawTeacher, 2013d). This means that the agreement has to be rendered frustrated to remove obligations by the injured party to perform the contractual agreement (LawTeacher, 2013d).

Case applications of the doctrine of frustration

The controversial debate on whether gadget usage should be unlimited for children or not is relevant nowadays because of the craze among parents to give children gadgets to play with. They fail to realise that giving gadgets to young children is not appropriate. Often, they end up regretting when their children suffer from slower development rates, addiction to gadget usage and a variety of other problems (American Academy of Pediatrics, 2017; Astri, 2017; Margalit, 2016).

ARTICLE 4

Taylor v. Caldwell (1863) 122 ER 309

One reason why discharge by frustration can take place is due to the destruction of a contract's physical subject matter (Birmingham, 1989). An applicable example of discharge by frustration because a contract's physical subject was destroyed is the Taylor v. Caldwell case. The doctrine of frustration was applied due to the destruction by burning of the contract's physical subject, a music hall (Surrey Gardens and Music Hall) for Caldwell, which was burnt shortly before it was scheduled to have concerts as stipulated by the contract (Trans-Lex.org, n. d.). When Surrey Gardens and Music Hall was destroyed beyond Caldwell's control, Caldwell ended up having no music hall to deliver the scheduled concerts despite being sued by Taylor, making it impossible to fulfil Caldwell's contract (Pillai and Bagavathi, 2013; Birmingham, 1989).

As the music hall's destruction was not within Caldwell's control and before the contract for concerts was to begin, Taylor lost his claim and his contract's original terms became impossible to fulfil (Pillai and Bagavathi, 2013; Pillai and Bagavathi, 2007; Birmingham, 1989). Both parties to the contract were discharged from absolute obligations to fulfil their original contracts under frustration despite the doctrine of absolute obligations because it became impossible with the music hall's destruction to fulfil their original contract and both parties were discharged from fulfilling their original contract effective from the moment the music hall was burnt and destroyed (LawTeacher, 2013c; Abbott, Pendlebury and Wardman, 2007). If contract obligations were followed, fulfilment of the contract would have been very different from the original contract terms due to the destruction of the music hall, allowing for a successful discharge by frustration from the original contract (LawTeacher, 2013c). Therefore, discharge by frustration to a contract when the original contract's physical subject is destroyed may be pleaded successfully (LawTeacher, 2013c).

Krell v. Henry [1903] 2 K.B. 740

Another reason why discharge by frustration can occur is the non-occurrence of an event essential to the formation of a contract (Lee and Detta, 2014). An example of a case law that can be applied to deal with frustration from the non-occurrence of an event is the Krell v. Henry case (Valpo.edu, 2013). The Krell v. Henry case had the defendant, C. S. Henry, being sued by the plaintiff, Paul Krell, for the usage of a flat at 56A, Pall Mall to view the processions for the British king's coronation, only to refuse to pay the plaintiff when the coronation processions did not occur as they were cancelled on account of the king's illness on the two days the processions were to take place (Valpo.edu, 2013). In this case, C. S. Henry wanted his liability to the plaintiff cancelled on account of the cancelled processions even when charged and sued for not paying the liability on the basis that the contract entered by him was without consideration due to the processions' cancellation (Valpo.edu, 2013).

On the basis of the contract's condition, the event of the coronation processions having been cancelled, Vaughan Williams L.J ruled that the non-occurrence of the contract's condition prevented the contract from being fulfilled and was a result of something which could not be anticipated by both parties to the contract (Valpo.edu, 2013). Relying on the Taylor v. Caldwell case, the Court of Appeal held that both parties to the contract assumed the coronation processions would occur as scheduled and pass under the flat booked by the defendant (Valpo.edu, 2013). The non-occurrence of an event which formed the basis of the original contract prevented the contract from being fulfilled to its original terms leading to discharge by frustration (Meyer and Lang, 2010; Arvind, 2017; Valpo.edu, 2013). This shows that contracts can be discharged by frustration through the non-occurrence of the event (Valpo.edu, 2013).

Horlock v. Beal [1916] 1 AC 486

Discharge by frustration due to changes in law can be pleaded (Gauge Data Solutions, 2017). An example of applying discharge by frustration to changes in law is the Horlock v. Beal case (Lee and Detta, 2014). This case involved changes in law due to the declaration of war by Britain on Germany on 4 August 1914 (Gauge Data Solutions, 2017). The declaration of war led to a ship detained in Germany with its sailors, leading to one of the detained sailors' wives suing to recover her husband's wages due to his service's termination by detention (Gauge Data Solutions, 2017; Gibson and Fraser, 2014; Mcelroy, 2014). The House of Lords held that no wages were to be provided for the husband since he ceased providing services (Mcelroy, 2014).

This case also discussed various dates to set discharge by frustration effective from the selected date, with the selected date for the contract's discharge by frustration due to changes in law initially determined to be 2 November 1914 as judges to the case assumed that the ship might be released prior to the ship's sailors' removal from the ship on this date, which would have allowed the contract's fulfilment (Gauge Data Solutions, 2017). Lords Atkinson and Shaw stated that the contract became impossible to fulfil effective from the ship's 4 August detention, especially since the detention of the ship or its crew was declared indefinite from 4 August and the subsequent inability to fulfil the contract was caused only by changes in law without the parties' fault (Gauge Data Solutions, 2017). In the end, it was determined by Lord Wrenbuey that the detained sailor could not fulfil his contract's original terms as the declaration of war and the ship's detention made fulfilment of the contract impossible, discharging the detained sailor from the contract by frustration effective from the declaration of war and the wife's appeal failed (Gauge Data Solutions, 2017; Gibson and Fraser, 2014). Also, no wages were given for the sailor since the contract was discharged, making it impossible to pay wages to the sailor (Gauge Data Solutions, 2017). This shows that if conditions to a contract cannot be fulfilled due to changes in law, the contract can be discharged (Gauge Data Solutions, 2017).

National Carriers Ltd v Panalpina (Northern) Ltd [1981] AC 675

Discharge by frustration can also occur because of physical obstructions, as displayed by the National Carriers Ltd v Panalpina (Northern) Ltd case (NADR, 2018). Nevertheless, this case shows that discharge by frustration due to physical obstructions could not occur only due to physical obstructions because of the contract's terms if the terms suggested that existing physical obstructions were insufficient to prevent the contract from being fulfilled (NADR, 2018). This case involved a warehouse, to be used by the contract's tenant after renting from and being leased by the landlord (NADR, 2018). The tenant was prevented from reaching the warehouse by another warehouse designated as a heritage site, with the warehouse leased to the tenant requiring Kingston Street to be accessed and the latter warehouse, located on Kingston Street and in a dangerous condition, preventing the former warehouse from being reached and used (NADR, 2018). Therefore, the warehouse leased to the tenant became unusable and the tenant appealed that his lease was frustrated (NADR, 2018).

Lord Wilberforce held that the physical obstruction to Kingston Street was anticipated by parties to the lease as lasting for a year or slightly longer, suggesting a possibility in renewing contractual obligations for the remaining three years the contract was to last based on its formation date of 1 January 1974, with the contract intending to last for ten years from 1 January 1974 based on its terms (NADR, 2018). In the end, the case was dismissed (NADR, 2018). This shows that discharge by frustration also applies to physical obstructions, but is inapplicable when the obstructions are not judged to be sufficiently serious in nature so as to prevent the contract from being completely fulfilled to its stipulated terms (NADR, 2018).

Fibrosa Spolka Akcyjna v Fairburn Lawson Combe Barbour Ltd [1943] AC 32

When the doctrine of frustration is applied, it will only apply to a contract effective from the contract's frustrating event and the moment of the frustrating event which caused the contract to be discharged by frustration (Lee and Detta, 2014). In the event a contract was discharged, money paid before the contract's frustrating event could not be refunded, but payments not yet paid when the frustrating event occurred and to be paid after the event could be cancelled (Stone, 2013). Therefore, obligations resulting from the contract before its frustrating event occurred are still valid unless there is total failure of consideration (Lee and Detta, 2014).

An example of this condition's applicability is the Fibrosa Spolka Akcyjna v Fairburn Lawson Combe Barbour Ltd case (Lee and Detta, 2014). This case had Fairburn Lawson Combe Barbour Ltd selling machinery to Fibrosa Spolka Akcyjna (Lawteacher, 2013b). When the delivery of machinery to Gdynia could not take place as stipulated in the contract due to Gdynia's occupation by Germany and war between Britain and Poland against Germany, discharging the contract by frustration, 1000 out of 1600 pounds paid by Fibrosa Spolka Akcyjna as deposit before the war was sued for recovery (Lawteacher, 2013b; Mckendrick, 2013).

The Court held that the contract's consideration failed and that money paid before the contract was frustrated was allowed to be recovered by Fibrosa Spolka Akcyjna (Mckendrick, 2013; Mitchell and Mitchell, 2008). This shows that without the total failure of consideration, obligations for a contract are still valid before its frustrating event set in (Lee and Detta, 2014).

Conclusion

In conclusion, the doctrine by frustration can be used to discharge a contract when an unforeseen event occurs outside the control of the contracting parties (Lawteacher, 2013e).

Discharge by frustration can occur because of the destruction of the contract's physical subject, the non-occurrence of the event essential to a contract's original terms, changes in law making it impossible to fulfil the original terms of the contract (Birmingham, 1989; Valpo.edu, 2013; Gauge Data Solutions, 2017; NADR, 2018).

Discharge by frustration can only be valid effective from the date of the frustrating event resulting in a total failure of consideration (NADR, 2018; Lee and Detta, 2014).

Collected Articles

REFERENCES

Collected Articles

Abbott, K., Pendlebury, N. and Wardman, K. (2007) Business Law. 8th Edition. London: Thomson Learning, p. 156.
[Online]. Available from: Google Books. https://tinyurl.com/43anjxdj [Accessed 19 October 2018].

Arvind, T. T. (2017) Contract Law. 1st Edition. New York: Oxford University Press, p. 280.
[Online]. Available from: Google Books. https://tinyurl.com/8pr79fdd [Accessed 19 October 2018].

Birmingham, R. L. (1989) "Why Is There Taylor v. Caldwell - Three Propositions about Impracticability", Faculty Articles and Papers, p. 6, 132.
[Online]. Available from: https://tinyurl.com/2a5mdzhu [Accessed 25 September 2018].

Gauge Data Solutions (2017) Horlock V. Beal.
[Online]. Available from: https://tinyurl.com/4ufexknm [Accessed 2 October 2018].

Gibson, A. and Fraser, D. (2014) Business Law 2014. Frenchs Forest: Pearson Australia, p. 533.
[Online]. Available from: Google Books. https://tinyurl.com/54p55s3b [Accessed 21 October 2018].

LawTeacher (2013a) Cutter v Powell - 1795.
[Online]. Available from: https://tinyurl.com/5n8tn7ex [Accessed 25 September 2018].

LawTeacher (2013b) Fibrosa SA v Fairbairn Lawson Combe Barbour Ltd [1943] AC 32.
[Online]. Available from: https://tinyurl.com/y4uxhh9j [Accessed 21 October 2018].

LawTeacher (2013c) Taylor V Caldwell [1863] 3 B&S 826 Case Summary.
[Online]. Available from: https://tinyurl.com/v8d3wkv6 [Accessed 6 October 2018].

ARTICLE 4 - References

LawTeacher (2013d) The doctrine of frustration.
[Online]. Available from: https://tinyurl.com/4rzhpvfh
[Accessed 14 October 2018].

LawTeacher (2013e) The theory of frustration in English Law.
[Online]. Available from: https://tinyurl.com/wjmycywn
[Accessed 20 October 2018].

Lee, M. P. and Detta, I. D. (2014) Business Law. 2nd Edition. Shah Alam: Oxford Fajar, pp. 223-231.

Mcelroy, R. G. (2014) Impossibility of Performance. 1st Paperback Edition. New York: Cambridge University Press, p. 152.
[Online]. Available from: Google Books. https://tinyurl.com/4bywc8zk
[Accessed 14 October 2018].

Mckendrick, E. (2013) Force Majeure and Frustration of Contract. 2nd Edition. Abingdon: Informa Law.
[Online]. Available from: Google Books. https://tinyurl.com/mf3sn53w
[Accessed 21 October 2018].

Meyer, L. and Lang, P. (2010) Non-performance and Remedies Under International Contract Law Principles and Indian Contract Law: A Comparative Survey of the UNIDROIT Principles of International Commercial Contracts, the Principles of European Contract Law, and Indian Statutory Contract Law. Frankfurt am Main: Internationaler Verlag der Wissenschaften, p. 95.
[Online]. Available from: Google Books. https://tinyurl.com/59d5b273
[Accessed 19 October 2018].

Mitchell, C. and Mitchell, P. (2008) Landmark Cases in the Law of Contract. 1st Edition. Portland: Hart Publishing.
[Online]. Available from: Google Books. https://tinyurl.com/4k3zjz9b
[Accessed 21 October 2018].

Collected Articles

NADR (2018) National Carriers Ltd v Panalpina (Northern) Ltd [1980] Int.Com.L.R. 12/11, pp. 5-18.
[Online]. Available from: https://tinyurl.com/bdfvchnt
[Accessed 7 October 2018].

Pillai, R. S. N. and Bagavathi (2013) Legal Aspect of Business (Mercantile Law Industrial and Company Laws). Reprint with Corrections. New Delhi: S. Chand & Company Pvt. Ltd. 7361, p. 141.
[Online]. Available from: Google Books. https://tinyurl.com/5vdta5nt
[Accessed 21 October 2018].

Pillai, R. S. N. and Bagavathi (2007) Business Law. Reprint. New Delhi: S. Chand & Company Pvt. Ltd. 7361, p. 89.
[Online]. Available from: Google Books. https://tinyurl.com/57smtpt8
[Accessed 11 October 2018].

Stone, R. (2013) Q&A Contract Law 2013-2014. 10th Edition. Abingdon: Routledge.
[Online]. Available from: Google Books. https://tinyurl.com/2v3dysv4
[Accessed 21 October 2018].

Trans-Lex.org (n. d.) Taylor and Another v. Caldwell and Another.
[Online]. Available from: https://tinyurl.com/nhb3fas3
[Accessed 2 October 2018].

Valpo.edu (2013) Krell v Henry.
[Online]. Available from: https://tinyurl.com/3m5rnt3k
[Accessed 28 September 2018].

ARTICLE 4 - References

Collected Articles

ARTICLE 5

Cashless Economy for Developing Countries: A case in Indian context

Introduction

This case study is done with the intention of looking at developing countries' usage of the cashless economy, in particular, the cashless economy's usage and context in India and other developing countries.

By definition, a cashless economy refers to the usage of cheques, electronic payments and debit and credit cards instead of cash (Maurya, 2019). Despite the higher frequency of financial dealings in developing countries still being done in cash, cashless transactions are becoming more common (Kumar et al, 2017).

Examples of developing countries using the cashless economy more frequently are India and Nigeria (Kumar et al, 2017; Abu, Bolarinwa and Akpoviroro, 2018). Recent initiatives to encourage a less-cash-society have paved the way for a cashless economy and increased its relevance to India and other developing countries (Kumar et al, 2017).

This report looks at the suitability of the cashless economy based on the context of India and other developing countries (Kumar et al, 2017; Abu, Bolarinwa and Akpoviroro, 2018).

ARTICLE 5

Impact of cashless economy on commercial and central banks

One impact of a cashless economy on commercial banks in India is the reduction in money spent by these banks in producing, printing and securing currency notes and coins in conjunction with the Reserve Bank of India, as payments are done electronically (Jain, 2017). A manual transaction in an Indian bank can cost Rs. 40 to 45, which is significantly more expensive than the Rs. 7 to 8 spent on online banking in India (Balaji and Balaji, 2017). Another consequence of the cashless economy on Indian commercial banks is that a cashless economy in India reduces the demand for cash among Indians (Kumar et al, 2017). This increases the cash deposited into Indian commercial banks and allows these banks to lend money out to other people, increasing the velocity of money with money being exchanged among more people (Kumar et al, 2017; Mishkin, 2019). Finally, a cashless economy can assist commercial banks in India save on expenses paid to cash operations and companies dealing with cash logistics (Kumar et al, 2017).

In the case of Nigeria, one effect of the cashless economy on the nation's commercial banks is the ability of the banks to provide better customer coverage and services (Abu, Bolarinwa and Akpoviroro, 2018). In addition, the banks are more profitable and able to conduct transactions more quickly, not to mention the fact that there is more money and liquidity for loans to needy people (Akara and Asekome, 2018). Zimbabwe, too, is moving towards the cashless economy, but it has some way to go before it can reap the benefits of this phenomenon (Nyoni and Bonga, 2017). The cashless economy's application to its commercial banks is not as efficient as expected and financial transaction are still considered to be high (Nyoni and Bonga, 2017). Another developing nation experiencing the effects of the cashless economy is Indonesia (Rahayu and Day, 2017). Here, commercial banks are working on promoting innovation in the Indonesian economy (Rahayu and Day, 2017). However, they have to contend with disruptive new entrants in the economy (Rahayu and Day, 2017; David and Gantori, 2018).

An effect of India's switch to a cashless economy on India's Central Bank, also known as the Reserve Bank of India, is that it eliminates the bank's liability in relation to holding cash in circulation (Harris and Barr, 2019; Kumar et al, 2017). This allows the Reserve Bank to save money spent on securing physical currency (Mandal, 2017). However, it means that should it go bankrupt, it will not be able to refund money to its depositers (Kumar et al, 2017). In addition, India's Central Bank, with a cashless economy, can avoid losses from counterfeit currency (Kumar et al, 2017). It must be noted that another consequence to the Reserve Bank of India of India's move towards a cashless economy is the adoption of "Payment

Banks" (Mandal, 2017). Also, the Reserve Bank, due to the adoption of a cashless economy in India, has also reduced cash circulation in the Indian economy in anticipation of a decrease in cash transactions in India (Mandal, 2017).

The Central Bank of Nigeria, in anticipation of the launch of a cashless economy, has provided mobile payment systems for cashless transactions (Adu, 2016). Another possible impact of the cashless economy on the Central Bank of Nigeria is the loss of the bank's monopoly on the Nigerian monetary supply (Elechi and Anthony, 2016). For Zimbabwe, a cashless economy will also reduce the monopoly of its national bank, the Reserve Bank of Zimbabwe, on the Zimbabwean monetary supply (Chirume, 2018). In addition, the Reserve Bank of Zimbabwe will have to amend its monetary policy to deal with financial technology usage with a cashless economy (Chirume, 2018). In Indonesia, an impact of the cashless economy on Bank Indonesia is that it has encouraged it to impose regulations related to payment system services, in anticipation of increased Indonesian usage of the cashless economy with financial technology (Mapa, 2019; Sudibyo et al, 2018). This is in addition to regulations made by Bank Indonesia to ensure Indonesians make electronic cashless transactions with security and confidence, increasing the usage of the cashless economy with electronic cashless transactions (Sudibyo et al, 2018).

Impact of being cashless on the economy of developing countries

---

For developing countries such as India, an anticipated impact of the cashless economy is the reduced appearance of black money in the national economy since black money requires physical cash to function (Meher, 2017; Agrawal, 2017). This can help in reducing criminal activities involving the economy (Agrawal, 2017).

Another outcome of the cashless economy is India's ability to deal with the crisis of demonetisation, given that demonetisation has encouraged the necessity for a cashless economy (Joseph, 2019; Roy, 2018). An added convenience is the use of cards rather than cash to conduct transactions (Brahma and Dutta, 2018). The move to a cashless economy in India has also resulted in the distribution of machines and cards to Indian farms to assist in conducting cashless transactions (Nataraj, 2017).

A cashless economy in India can also block the likelihood of a parallel economy from using secret activities to obtain money, which reduces the likelihood of tax evasion (Kumar et al, 2017). Another positive effect is that a more accurate assessment of India's GDP can be made, leading to income equalities being reduced (Kumar et al, 2017). The reduced costs to India's economy with a cashless economy and debit cards replacing cash transactions can also provide a beneficial impact to the economy, with reduced deficit and less of India's GDP spent on maintaining cash (Kumar et al, 2017). This is in addition to the reduction of corruption in India which can be anticipated with a cashless economy (Omar et al, 2019). The final impact of the cashless economy on India is that by eliminating cash, it can reduce fears of anticipated losses caused by risks involved in holding cash (Kumar et al, 2017).

Where Nigeria is concerned, an effect of implementing a cashless economy is the reduction of corruption by eliminating cash transactions to assist in exposing corrupt transactions and reducing local corruption (Omar et al, 2019). In addition, it results in the setting up of affordable financial systems, the reduction of barriers hindering Nigerians from participating in financial transactions, enhanced customer satisfaction and reduced risks and costs associated with using cash (Adu, 2016; Abu, Bolarinwa and Akpoviroro, 2018). A survey involving Nigerians found that a cashless economy will reduce risks related to carrying cash (Okuma, Nwoko and Obialor, 2019). It can also help increase foreign investment in Nigeria (Okuma, Nwoko and Obialor, 2019).

In the case of Zimbabwe, the cashless economy has resulted in improved economic growth and more tax collection in the nation (Nyoni and Bonga, 2017). Another effect has been a stabilization of the country's economic growth as a result of controlled inflation (Nyoni and Bonga, 2017). The cashless economy also gives

Zimbabwe the opportunity to reduce corruption and eliminate criminal activities related to cash possession (Nyoni and Bonga, 2017).

In Indonesia, the increased presence of the cashless economy has resulted in an anticipated increase in patterns of using electronic payment machines and e-commerce in the country (Sudibyo et al, 2018).

ARTICLE 5

Analyse the possibilities of a cashless economy

A cashless economy is possible in India because of measures taken by the nation to encourage online financial transactions such as Ola money and through the "Digital India" campaign (Singhraul and Garwal, 2018; Pal, Tiwari and Khandelwal, 2019). Also, the usage of frontier technologies such as National Unified Unstructured Supplementary Services Data by the Reserve Bank of India has made the adoption of a cashless economy more likely by allowing activities such as mobile banking (Gandhi, 2016). In fact, there is statistical evidence that India is ready for a cashless economy.

In a study by Sharma and Agarwal (2018), 24% of Indians involved in the study strongly agreed and 38% of Indians involved in the study agreed with the question titled "Do you think India is completely ready for cashless economy?" (Sharma and Agarwal, 2018). The increased value and quantity of mobile banking and mobile wallet transactions in the aftermath of demonetization, through increased usage of non-cash transactions such as mobile banking and mobile wallets, is another sign that India is ready for a cashless economy (Rajasree and Vijayan, 2018).

This is in addition to the affordable costs and convenience of e-payments in India, resulting in the fact that e-payments are being used more frequently in India and making India more ready for a cashless economy with a more frequent usage of e-payments (Srikrishnan, 2017).

The cashless economy is also a possibility in India given the assistance of using the Unified Payments Interface for financial transactions through more secure privacy and an increased adoption of mobile phones for people making financial transactions in India (Gandhi, 2016) and the launching of flagship programs intended to transform India into a digital economy and a cashless economy with financial literacy and increased banking literacy among the Indian population (Bansal, 2017). Even in the rural areas of India, the implementation of a cashless economy has become more likely because of the digitalization and the changing consumption patterns with potential of several Indian villages, making India more ready for a cashless economy (Thomas and Krishnamurthi, 2017). In addition, demonetization in India has also increased the likelihood of a cashless economy in India by eliminating the economic constraints to a cashless economy in India such as black money and tax evasion (Nagdev et al, 2018).

The cashless economy is a possibility in other developing countries such as Nigeria and Zimbabwe as well (Elechi and Anthony, 2016; Nyoni and Bonga, 2017). In Nigeria, efforts have been made by the Central Bank of Nigeria to get payments done electronically instead of by cash (Elechi and Anthony, 2016). In Zimbabwe, efforts have been made to get Zimbabwe to become a cashless economy with the usage of technology and financial literacy programs (Nyoni and Bonga, 2017). Also, using e-money as an alternative to cash has been expected to stabilize the Zimbabwean economy's financial sector and growth, which should encourage the likelihood of cashless economic activities (Nyoni and Bonga, 2017). Technology has also been used to make the cashless economy a possibility in Indonesia as well by allowing financial transactions to be done with electronic money in increasing amounts yearly (Xena and Rahadi, 2019). This can be assisted by further infrastructure development in Indonesia for electronic money usage and by regulations enforcing such usage for transactions involving tolls, parking areas and online vehicle usage (Xena and Rahadi, 2019).

However, one reason why a cashless economy may have problems thriving in India, especially in less urbanized and unreached markets in India, is because of the low percentage (26%) of India's population with Internet accessibility (Singhraul and Garwal, 2018). This is in addition to a lack of awareness about digital banking, Internet bill payments, mobile transactions and credit and debit card transactions in India (Singhraul and Garwal, 2018). The prevalence of cash usage in India's rural areas and bigger cities and a fear of advanced technology usage have been found to prevent people from adopting a cashless economy (Garg and Panchal, 2017; Sarkar, 2017). It is hoped this problem can be solved by India's 'Aadhaar Pay' initiative, which will allow financial transactions to be done with just the fingerprints of poorer people, and the usage of the Unique Identification Authority of India (UIDAI) to allow poorer people to conduct their transactions without cards or smartphones (Varshney, Bhatia and Gupta, 2017; Ravi, 2017).

Another barrier preventing the adoption of a cashless economy in India is the dominance of small retailers (Garg and Panchal, 2017). These retailers lack the resources to invest in an electronic payment infrastructure for a cashless economy (Garg and Panchal, 2017). In addition, small retailers in India also fear losing money with cashless transactions and prefer transactions with cash (Chattopadhyay, 2018; Garg and Panchal, 2017). Another concern is that the Indian banking infrastructure may not be well-equipped to handle a cashless economy unless major changes are implemented, with mobile device accessibility and network connectivity being needed for the digital transactions (Sarkar, 2017; Kumar et al, 2017). Without such accessibility connectivity, a cashless economy is likely to falter (Kumar et al, 2017).

Demonetization in India and the resultant steady reduction in a preference for cash transactions did not last long, and a reliance on cash in increased or fluctuating frequencies has become the norm (Maiti, Hemachandra and Sharma, 2019). This makes it difficult for the Indian government to impose a cashless economy over India without considering potential opposition (Maiti,

Hemachandra and Sharma, 2019; Ramakumar, 2018). Such opposition has to be dealt with before any progress can take place (Ramakumar, 2018; Garg and Panchal, 2017). The government has to give guarantees that cashless transactions are safe, certain and easier than transactions with cash (Garg and Panchal, 2017). In addition, Indian banks have to upgrade their cyber security, as digital information related to these transactions can be lost without adequate cyber security (Kumar et al, 2017).

Nigeria has similar problems when trying to adopt a cashless economy (Omar et al, 2019; Elechi and Anthony, 2016). For example, the infrastructure associated with Internet connection and reliable electricity supply has been found to be poorly equipped for handling cashless transactions (Omar et al, 2019). In addition, the rural population of Nigeria is inadequately educated and too illiterate to use a cashless economy (Omar et al, 2019). There is the possibility that Nigerian people are generally more used to having cash than going without cash (Omar et al, 2019). It is also quite evident that cybercrime affecting online transactions can stand in the way of a cashless economy in the country (Omar et al, 2019).

For Zimbabwe, the possibility of adopting a cashless economy has been found to be restricted by less developed infrastructure such as insufficient telecommunication networks (Nyoni and Bonga, 2017). Also, Zimbabwean consumers and business enterprises tend to lack knowledge about the cashless economy's benefits and financial transactions (Nyoni and Bonga, 2017). In Indonesia, the population tends to use cash for financial transactions as opposed to credit cards and virtual money (Sudibyo et al, 2018; Syahadiyanti and Subriadi, 2018). Given such circumstances, the implementation of the cashless economy in Indonesia faces substantial hurdles (Syahadiyanti and Subriadi, 2018). This is exacerbated by a lack of understanding about using electronic payment machines and by the fact that non-cash payments constituted only a small percentage (31%) of total consumer payments in Indonesia in 2013 (Sudibyo et al, 2018).

Conclusion

In conclusion, the adoption of a cashless economy is possible in India because of Indian government initiatives to encourage online financial transactions, increased e-payment usage, technology, mobile banking, and mobile wallet transactions (Singhraul and Garwal, 2018; Srikrishnan, 2017; Gandhi, 2016; Rajasree and Vijayan, 2018). Conversely, the lack of Internet access, the prevalence of cash transactions and a lack of resources among the small retailers who dominate India's economy can hinder a cashless economy (Singhraul and Garwal, 2018; Garg and Panchal, 2017). Another barrier to India's adoption of a cashless economy is the lack of adequate technological development to allow banks to conduct cashless economic transactions (Sarkar, 2017). Nevertheless, it can be expected that India will transition into a cashless economy in the future (Singhraul and Garwal, 2018).

For other developing countries such as Nigeria, it can be concluded that a cashless economy is possible, despite its poor infrastructure (Omar et al, 2019). The same can be inferred for Zimbabwe (Nyoni and Bonga, 2017). In the case of Indonesia, it can be said that, despite certain issues, it is on its path to a cashless economy, with regulations enforcing and encouraging the usage of electronic money, together with infrastructure development (Xena and Rahadi, 2019; Sudibyo et al, 2018).

Collected Articles

REFERENCES

Collected Articles

Abu, Z., Bolarinwa, K. I. and Akpoviroro, K. S. (2018) Evaluation of Prospect and Challenges of Cashless Policy. The Case of Commercial Banks in Nigeria, Financial Markets, Institutions and Risks, 2 (4), pp. 92-100.
[Online]. Available from: https://tinyurl.com/yc5zbh63
[Accessed 3 February 2020].

Adu, C. A. (2016) Cashless Policy And Its Effects On The Nigerian Economy, European Journal of Business, Economics and Accountancy, 4 (2), pp. 81-88.
[Online]. Available from: https://tinyurl.com/mrx95njj
[Accessed 3 February 2020].

Agrawal, R. K. (2017) Study on Introduction of Cashless Economy in India: Benefits & Challenges, International Journal of Research in Management, Economics and Commerce, 7 (12), December, pp. 187-189.
[Online]. Available from: https://tinyurl.com/3ue8e6z8
[Accessed 18 January 2020].

Akara, C. K. and Asekome, M. O. (2018) Cashless Policy and Commercial Banks' Profitability In Nigeria, Advances in Social Sciences Research Journal, March, 5 (3), pp. 395-406.
[Online]. Available from: https://tinyurl.com/ms5jzap2
[Accessed 3 February 2020].

Balaji, K. C. and Balaji, K. (2017) A Study of Demonetization And Its Impact On Cashless Transactions, International Journal of Advanced Scientific Research & Development, March, 4 (3, I), pp. 58-64.
[Online]. Available from: https://tinyurl.com/5cvn7x8h
[Accessed 26 January 2020].

Basu, A. (2018) The inclusion factors towards a cashless economy, International Journal of Commerce and Management Research, September, 4 (5), pp. 81-84.
[Online]. Available from: https://tinyurl.com/4f589spa
[Accessed 18 January 2020].

ARTICLE 5 - References

Brahma, A. and Dutta, R. (2018) Cashless Transactions and Its Impact - A Wise Move Towards Digital India, International Journal of Scientific Research in Computer Science, Engineering and Information Technology, March-April, 3 (3), pp. 14-28.
[Online]. Available from: https://tinyurl.com/yc6ce59j
[Accessed 27 January 2020].

Chattopadhyay, S. (2018) Awareness and Participation of Small Retail Businesses in Cashless Transactions: An Empirical Study, Management Dynamics in the Knowledge Economy, June, 2, pp. 209-225.
[Online]. Available from: https://tinyurl.com/5xnermxb
[Accessed 29 January 2020].

Chirume, A. T. (2018) Financial Technology, Digital Currency and Monetary Policy in Zimbabwe, pp. 1-8.
[Online]. Available from: https://tinyurl.com/z22p7khm
[Accessed 8 February 2020].

David, J. and Gantori, S. (2018) The road to cashless societies, pp. 1-35.
[Online]. Available from: https://tinyurl.com/njmzsd2a
[Accessed 10 February 2020].

Elechi, A. C. and Anthony, R. (2016) Cashless Policy in Nigeria and Its Socio-Economic Impacts, Public Policy and Administration Research, 6 (10), pp. 16-22.
[Online]. Available from: https://tinyurl.com/3k65pb6p
[Accessed 4 February 2020].

Gandhi, R. (2016) R Gandhi: Pioneering best practices in banking – India's record, pp. 1-7.
[Online]. Available from: https://tinyurl.com/3fkursnt
[Accessed 18 January 2020].

Collected Articles

Garg, P. and Panchal, M. (2017) Study on Introduction of Cashless Economy in India 2016: Benefits & Challenge's, IOSR Journal of Business and Management, April, 19 (4, ii), pp. 116-120.
[Online]. Available from: (PDF) Study on Introduction of Cashless Economy in India 2016: Benefits & Challenge's (researchgate.net)
[Accessed 28 January 2020].

Harris, A. and Barr, M. S. (2019) Central Bank of the Future, U of Michigan Public Law Research Paper No. 1, Center on Finance, Law & Policy, University of Michigan, Ann Arbor, pp. 1-20.
[Online]. Available from: https://tinyurl.com/3yswstba
[Accessed 18 January 2020].

Jain, M. (2017) Making towards a Cashless Economy: Challenges and Opportunities for India, Indian Journal of Applied Research, January, 7 (1), pp. 722-723.
[Online]. Available from: https://tinyurl.com/5n8d46a9
[Accessed 18 January 2020].

Joseph, M. A. (2019) Impact of Demonetisation on Retail Sector, Journal of The Gujarat Research Society, October, 21 (5), pp. 231-242.
[Online]. Available from: https://tinyurl.com/yc67c22j
[Accessed 19 January 2020].

Kumar, A., Dua, V., Sharma, P., Jain, S. and Garg, P. (2017) Cashless Economy For Developing Countries: A Case In Indian Context, Flame International Case Conference, June, pp. 1-9.
[Online]. Available from: https://tinyurl.com/2femh5rw
[Accessed 16 January 2020].

Maiti, S. S., Hemachandra, N. and Sharma, A. K. (2019) Cash preference in India: Empirical methods and findings, Journal of Payments Strategy & Systems, Summer, 13 (2), pp. 165-176.
[Online]. Available from: https://tinyurl.com/4ayrpxwt
[Accessed 27 January 2020].

ARTICLE 5 - References

Mandal, P. K. (2017) Problems and Prospects of Cashless India, New Delhi: Educreation Publishing, pp. 1-51.
[Online]. Available from: Google Books. https://tinyurl.com/y8pdh24w [Accessed 18 January 2020].

Mapa, N. (2019) Indonesia: Central bank holds rates steady, trims reserve requirement.
[Online]. Available from: https://tinyurl.com/mszxsfz7 [Accessed 9 February 2020].

Maurya, P. (2019) Cashless Economy and Digitalization, Proceedings of 10th International Conference on Digital Strategies for Organizational Success, January, pp. 710-715.
[Online]. Available from: https://tinyurl.com/3r7k82hp [Accessed 15 January 2020].

Meher, B. K. (2017) Impact of Demonetization on NPA Position of Indian Banks, International Journal of Advanced Scientific Research and Engineering Trends, 2 (1), August, pp. 1-8.
[Online]. Available from: https://tinyurl.com/mkxsbb29 [Accessed 15 January 2020].

Mishkin, F. S. (2019) The Economics of Money, Banking and Financial Markets, 12th Edition, Harlow: Pearson Education Limited, pp. 532-545.

Nagdev, K., Kumar, P., Rajesh, A. and Kumar, S. (2018) Measuring demonetisation: a path towards the cashless India, Int. J. Public Sector Performance Management, 4 (1), pp. 114-132.
[Online]. Available from: https://tinyurl.com/28mdy775 [Accessed 28 January 2020].

Nataraj, G. (2017) Demonetisation and its Impact, New Delhi: Indian Institute of Public Administration, pp. 1-19.
[Online]. Available from: https://tinyurl.com/3732zuv8 [Accessed 1 February 2020].

Collected Articles

Nyoni, T. and Bonga, W. G. (2017) Cashless Transacting Economy: A Necessary Evil for Development! A Zimbabwean Scenario!, Journal of Economics and Finance, April, 2 (4), pp. 1-10.
[Online]. Available from: https://tinyurl.com/3hys5u29
[Accessed 4 February 2020].

Okuma, N. C., Nwoko, C. N. J. and Obialor, C. B.-M. (2019) Causal Relationship Between Technologies Of Cashless Policy And Agricultural Sector Output In Nigeria, Global Journal of Applied, Management and Social Sciences, January, 16, pp. 105-119.
[Online]. Available from: https://tinyurl.com/yfs3eybc
[Accessed 8 February 2020].

Omar, A., Rana, A., Naziruddin, A., Zalina, Z. and Mazhar, H. K. (2019) The Future Of Corruption In The Era Of Cashless Society, Humanities & Social Sciences Reviews, August, 7 (2), pp. 454-458.
[Online]. Available from: https://tinyurl.com/yc57b64b
[Accessed 2 February 2020].

Pal, A., Tiwari, C. K. and Khandelwal, T. (2019) India Towards a Cashless Economy, in: Behl, A. and Nayak, S. (eds.) Maintaining Financial Stability in Times of Risk and Uncertainty. Hershey: IGI Global, pp. 138-156.
[Online]. Available from: Google Books. https://tinyurl.com/2a5crsph
[Accessed 23 January 2020].

Rahayu, R. and Day, J. (2017) Determinant Factors of E-commerce Adoption by SMEs in Developing Country: Evidence from Indonesia, Eurasian Business Review, 7, pp. 25-41.
[Online]. Available from: https://tinyurl.com/2db9umx6
[Accessed 9 February 2020].

Rajasree, K. R. and Vijayan, V. (2018) Branchless Banking In India, International Journal of Pure and Applied Mathematics, 118 (20), pp. 4221-4226.
[Online]. Available from: https://tinyurl.com/6ndsw5v3
[Accessed 26 January 2020].

ARTICLE 5 - References

Ramakumar, R. (2018) A Nation In the Queue: On How Demonetisation Wrecked the Economy and Livelihoods in India, in: Ramakumar, R. (ed.) Note-Bandi: Demonetisation and India's Elusive Chase for Black Money, New Delhi: Oxford University Press, 1st Edition.
[Online]. Available from: Google Books. https://tinyurl.com/5abk3mj3
[Accessed 28 January 2020].

Ravi, C. S. (2017) Digital payments system and rural India: A review of transaction to cashless economy, International Journal of Commerce and Management Research, May, 3 (5), pp. 169-173.
[Online]. Available from: https://tinyurl.com/5ctujauf
[Accessed 19 January 2020].

Roy, P. (2018) The Digitization Wave in India: A SWOC Analysis with Special Reference to the Demonetization and a Leap towards Cashless Economy, IRA-International Journal of Management & Social Sciences, January, 10 (1), pp. 54-62.
[Online]. Available from: https://tinyurl.com/522mzpva
[Accessed 20 January 2020].

Sarkar, S. (2017) Alternate Channels of Banks and Digital/ Cashless Economy: A Micro-Analytical Study on the Awareness and Use of Various Alternate Channels in Guwahati Metropolitan Region, International Journal of Banking, Risk and Insurance, 5 (2), September, pp. 54-65.
[Online]. Available from: https://tinyurl.com/yzws3nka
[Accessed 23 January 2020].

Sharma, A. and Agarwal, H. (2018) Study of Recent Developments Related to Cashless Commerce in India, Journal of Commerce and Trade, October, 13 (2), pp. 66-71.
[Online]. Available from: https://tinyurl.com/bdb8cmtb
[Accessed 23 January 2020].

Collected Articles

Shamshadali, P., Fidha, C. P. and Syamijth, C. (2018) Evaluation of cashless economy concept in Indian scenario, Indian Journal of Economics and Development, December, 6 (12), pp. 1-7.
[Online]. Available from: https://tinyurl.com/yyknzcdv
[Accessed 26 January 2020].

Singhraul, B. P. and Garwal, Y. S. (2018) Cashless Economy – Challenges and Opportunities in India, Pacific Business Review International, 10 (9), March, pp. 54-63.
[Online]. Available from: https://tinyurl.com/2et8bdh8
[Accessed 16 January 2020].

Srikrishnan, S. (2017) Demonetization, the Movement to an Electronic Payments System and the inch towards Full Financial Inclusion in the Indian Economy, Annandale-on-Hudson: Bard College, pp. 1-94.
[Online]. Available from: https://tinyurl.com/4dkhuzsb
[Accessed 1 February 2020].

Sudibyo, S. D., Maarif, M. S., Sukmawati, A. and Affandi, M. J. (2018) Analysis Of Factors Affecting People's Behavior In Using Electronic Payment Instruments, Jurnal Organisasi dan Manajemen, September, 14 (2), pp. 108-119.
[Online]. Available from: https://tinyurl.com/4jshex4f
[Accessed 9 February 2020].

Syahadiyanti, L. and Subriadi, A. P. (2018) Diffusion of Innovation Theory Utilization Online Financial Transaction: Literature Review, International Journal of Economics and Financial Issues, 8 (3), pp. 219-226.
[Online]. Available from: https://tinyurl.com/ykhcmv5w
[Accessed 17 February 2020].

Thomas, S. and Krishnamurthi, G. (2017) Cashless Rural Economy – A Dream or Reality ? Jharkhand Journal of Development and Management Studies, June, 15 (2), pp. 7269-7281.
[Online]. Available from: https://tinyurl.com/rekp5txk
[Accessed 23 January 2020].

ARTICLE 5 - References

Uke, L. (2017) Demonetization and its Effects in India, SSRG International Journal of Economics and Management Studies, February, 4 (2), pp. 18-22.
[Online]. Available from: https://tinyurl.com/2s4fkefp
[Accessed 19 January 2020].

Varshney, N., Bhatia, M. and Gupta, H. (2017) Impact of Cashless Economy in the development of India: Drives and challenges, Proceedings of International Conference 2017, pp. 1-2.
[Online]. Available from: https://tinyurl.com/39z5px6a
[Accessed 19 January 2020].

Xena, P. and Rahadi, R. A. (2019) Adoption Of E-Payment To Support Small Medium Enterprise Payment System: A Conceptualised Model, International Journal of Accounting, Finance and Business, March, 4 (18), pp. 32-41.
[Online]. Available from: https://tinyurl.com/3ftb9edj
[Accessed 9 February 2020].

Collected Articles

ARTICLE 6

Exams offer little more than a test of a student's ability to sit in exams.

Should schools *abolish* examinations for students?

Introduction

This article discusses whether examinations for students should be abolished or not and my opinion on this topic (Tambawal, 2013; Yesuiah, 2017; Tait, 2015; Guldin, 2009; Wong, Loh and Williams, 2008; Torgerson, 1944).

Over the years, there have been statements that are related to the need to abolish examinations based on several reasons (Guldin, 2009). The main reason is the stress they create in students, which affects their lives (Guldin, 2009). Also, the suitability of examinations for preparing students for the real world and defining the intelligence of their candidates are factors that need to be looked at (Yesuiah, 2017; Tait, 2015). Several studies have been carried out to prove the negative impact of examinations on students' lives (Tambawal, 2013; Guldin, 2009).

Conversely, there is evidence to indicate the benefits of examinations (Wong, Loh and Williams, 2008; Bergen and Lane, 2014; Torgerson, 1944). For example, students can gain proficiency through studying hard, examinations can promote critical thinking, and there are potentially negative consequences of a world where examinations are abolished (Wong, Loh and Williams, 2008; Bergen and Lane, 2014; Torgerson, 1944).

Content

One reason why examinations should be abolished is that malpractice within examinations can occur during examination days and marking (Tambawal, 2013). By definition, malpractice is intentional wrongdoing with the aim of favouritism (Tambawal, 2013). Examination malpractice can be caused through leakage by examination authorities, parental threats with punishment and harm, the pressure of stress on students and teachers, lack of control due to remote distances from examination centres to the examination staff's homes and insufficient school [and house] provisions that result in an inability to study and practice for examinations (Tambawal, 2013). As stated by Tambawal (2013), malpractice reduces integrity in the examination system and causes the loss of examination system credibility (Tambawal, 2013). In contrast, non-examination activities will reduce examination stress that causes students to cheat, especially with the high stakes and difficult examination material involved in several examinations provided to students (Guldin, 2009; Tambawal, 2013).

One of the most important factors that contribute to whether examinations should be abolished or not is whether they will succeed or fail in preparing students for the real world, even if the students get straight A's for every examination they take (Yesuiah, 2017). Edison (n. d.), as cited by Djemil (2016), stated, "Tomorrow is my exam but I don't care, a single paper can't decide my future." In fact, many people only achieved the success they were known for later in their lives and after repeated failures (Farson, 2007). Achieving beyond a 'pass' in examinations isn't everything in life when there are many more skills to learn unless examination results are needed to be promoted further in life and these skills aren't necessarily going to be tested in every examination that you take (Yesuiah, 2017). However, this can lead to a refusal by students to study and hence, their study attitude degenerates for the worse as they refuse to study seriously until failure in the future (Wong, Loh and Williams, 2008).

Another piece of very important evidence as to why examinations aren't everything in life comes from the fact that intelligence alone cannot be solely defined by examinations (Tait, 2015). The British system of public examinations is believed to have separated the more intelligent pupils from less intelligent ones, but it is apparent that this opinion only encourages a misconception that students who do well in their examinations are always intelligent and those who don't, aren't (Tait, 2015). Intelligence is actually the ability to understand and apply knowledge to a higher level and examinations don't define it (Tait, 2015). It must be noted that, depending on circumstances, career choices are not solely defined by examination results, especially if the student does not have the initiative to find a career or success that reflects his examination results (Yesuiah, 2017).

ARTICLE 6

The main reason why teachers may be in favour of abolishing examinations, at least in my opinion, is because of the stress that occurs in students as a result of examinations [especially for naturally weaker students] (Guldin, 2009). This stress can lead to depression, mood swings, and changes in and daily habits (Guldin, 2009). In some cases, students may even experience eating habit changes, resort to excessive drug consumption [through Adderall and Ritalin usage] to stay awake for their revision and examination days, and activity deprivation (Guldin, 2009).

In Britain, examination stress had been exacerbated by the increase in tuition fees for university since 2011, which increased the pressure on students to obtain good examination grades in order to avoid the possibility of a resit (Pressure of exams, 2011). Increased pressure and stress from examinations can lead to self-harm when it becomes too much for stressed students to tolerate, especially when weighed-down by persistent diseases and health problems (Pressure of exams, 2011; Jernelöv et al, 2009). Students in a world without examinations will be less stressed without the need to study for examinations (Wong, Loh and Williams, 2008). Nevertheless, despite the stress associated with examinations, they have potential in improving how students learn their school material, which, in my opinion, makes up for the stress associated with examinations since hard work and effective study and work skills are more important than just resting for pleasure (Bergen and Lane, 2014).

On the other hand, there are reasons why examinations should not be abolished (Wong, Loh and Williams, 2008). Firstly, without examinations, there is a loss of incentive for students to revise and prepare relevant information for the future (Wong, Loh and Williams, 2008). Secondly, in relation to the gender factor, a non-examination system could affect boys more negatively than their female counterparts (Brooke, 2010; Topping and Maloney, 2005). The change from exam-only O' Levels to GCSEs with coursework may put them on the backfoot due to the possibility that prolonged hours of coursework may not be their strength, compared to girls (Brooke, 2010; Topping and Maloney, 2005). Examinations may make them more motivated to study hard and achieve success on par with their female classmates (Brooke, 2010; Topping and Maloney, 2005). Thirdly, universities will find processing student-entry a complicated procedure if there is no proof of examination performance to judge who is qualified and who is not (Torgerson, 1944). It will require replacing traditional rules for admittance with hitherto untried arrangements, which could be chaotic and time-consuming (Torgerson, 1944).

Also, teachers will find the need to teach their lessons seriously reduced as they are less likely to consider teaching lessons effectively through marking [and preparing] homework and assignments without examinations (Wong, Loh and Williams, 2008). In his hypothetical scenario, the future of a student generation trained in this system will not be beneficial as its members will perform poorly in their jobs and having to remedy the scenario with examinations again will be needed since students won't be studying hard enough for the future (Wong, Loh and Williams, 2008). To make things worse, most teachers still around to teach by the time will have been exposed to teaching without preparing examinations for students, which makes adaptability to the solution difficult for them (Wong, Loh and Williams, 2008).

The right examinations, when done properly, can be beneficial for students (Bergen and Lane, 2014). For example, an examination that focuses more on understanding, critical thinking and practical hands-on skills can be more beneficial than the typical examination that only requires memorization and the answering of multiple-choice questions without preparing for real life usage (Bergen and Lane, 2014).

Similarly, increased efforts spent by students to study for their examinations and from teachers in ensuring the relevance and usefulness of examination content for the future are also important (Bergen and Lane, 2014). Teachers can ensure that they prepare students for the future by helping them do well in examinations (Bergen and Lane, 2014). Students, in turn, will learn to appreciate the value of examinations as more than just tools with which to merely understand the subjects they are taking or getting only relevant qualifications for future jobs (Bergen and Lane, 2014). The authorities can do this by changing the scope of the examinations to cover each subject's more relevant aspects, skills and formats and prove the usefulness in them (Bergen and Lane, 2014).

Another benefit of examinations is the elimination of the possibility of cheating, plagiarism and ghost writing without being punished when caught (Bergen and Lane, 2014). Students cannot cheat by, for example, bringing in resources for referencing into the exam room (Bergen and Lane, 2014). This forces them to study hard in order to succeed while instilling a sense of integrity in them (Bergen and Lane, 2014). Studying and preparing also reinforce their memorisation abilities (Bergen and Lane, 2014). When combined with the relevant qualifications proven by examinations, it makes the approval of job qualifications through skills possible (Bergen and Lane, 2014).

Claims by supporters of coursework, that examinations do not strengthen specific living and academic skills such as critical thinking and analysis, can be countered with the argument that examinations are useful in testing knowledge and proficiency in a variety of skills (Bergen and Lane, 2014).

As memory and proficiency are not likely to be tested in a non-examination approach since students can ask for and collect information from their parents, their school notes or the media, it is apparent that examinations are irreplaceable, especially in the proficiency aspect (Bergen and Lane, 2014). Without proficiency in the required qualifications and lessons, critical thinking is useless in an occupation (Bergen and Lane, 2014).

Conclusion

To sum up, examinations should not be abolished (Bergen and Lane, 2014; Wong, Loh and Williams, 2008).

As mentioned, the proficiency provided by examinations in developing skills through studying is a major plus and will not be possible even if coursework replaced abolished examinations (Bergen and Lane, 2014). In a scenario without examinations, the negative consequences in the outcome stated by Arthur Williams can become a possibility (Wong, Loh and Williams, 2008).

Finally, examinations can be structured to promote critical thinking, contrary to the thinking of some (Bergen and Lane, 2014). The stress factor aside, effectiveness in defining student intelligence and in preparing students for the future make examinations relevant (Guldin, 2009; Tait, 2015; Yesuiah, 2017).

REFERENCES

Collected Articles

'Pressure of exams leaves teens suffering from mental illness', Telegraph, (2011, 25 August).
[Online]. Available from: https://tinyurl.com/y6sc5ky4
[Accessed 19 July 2017].

Bergen, P. V. and Lane, R. (2014) 'Exams might be stressful, but they improve learning', Theconversation.com, 18 December.
[Online]. Available from: https://tinyurl.com/27dssppt
[Accessed 19 July 2017].

Brooke, C. (2010) 'Exams for boys and coursework for girls: Test board considers separate GCSEs for the sexes', Daily Mail, 18 June.
[Online]. Available from: https://tinyurl.com/3bvrfb4m
[Accessed 15 July 2017].

Djemil, B. (2016) Why Exams Should Be Abolished From Schools.
[Online]. Available from: https://tinyurl.com/mtrswnxv
[Accessed 12 July 2017].

Farson, R. (2007) The Case of Failure: Risk, Innovation, and Engagement, in: Blankstein, A. M., Cole, R.W. and Houston, P.D. (eds.) Engaging EVERY Learner, pp. 173-192.
[Online]. Available from: Google Books. https://tinyurl.com/2ur7at87
[Accessed 13 July 2017].

Guldin, W. (2009) 'Final exams causes students to have stress, bad habits', TheManEater, 8 May.
[Online]. Available from: https://tinyurl.com/59mn4yeb
[Accessed 13 July 2017].

Jernelöv, S., Höglund, C. O., Axelsson, J., Axén, J., Grönneberg, R., Grunewald, J., Stierna, P. and Lekander, M. (2009) Effects of examination stress on psychological responses, sleep and allergic symptoms in atopic and non-atopic students, "Int J Behav Med." (journal), 16 (4), pp. 305-310.
[Online]. Available from: https://tinyurl.com/4dnn9et8
[Accessed 9 July 2017].

ARTICLE 6 - References

Tait, P. (2015) 'Intelligence cannot be defined by exams', Telegraph, 17 June. *[Online]. Available from: https://tinyurl.com/59xmkrj7 [Accessed 12 July 2017].*

Tambawal, M. U. (2013) Examination Malpractices, Causes, Effects and Solutions, pp. 2-8, *[Online]. Available from: https://tinyurl.com/bdd4ekvm [Accessed 12 July 2017].*

Topping, K. J. and Maloney, S. (2005) The RoutledgeFalmer Reader in Inclusive Education. Abingdon: RoutledgeFalmer, p. 87. *[Online]. Available from: Google Books. https://tinyurl.com/294rcce8 [Accessed 9 July 2017].*

Torgerson, T. L. (1944) Examinations Are Important, The American Journal of Nursing, October, 44 (10), pp. 985-987. *[Online]. Available from: https://tinyurl.com/3m28twfz [Accessed 12 July 2017].*

Wong, J., Loh, F. and Williams, A. (2008) Why Examinations Are Important, in: Williams, A. [eds.] New Model English Essays. Singapore: Equus Publishing Pte. Ltd., pp. 36-39.

Yesuiah, S. (2017) 'Success In Life Not defined by exam results', The Star Online, 9 April. *[Online]. Available from: https://tinyurl.com/5bat34ku [Accessed 15 July 2017].*

Collected Articles

ARTICLE 7

Differences in Family Life and romantic relations between the 20th and 21st centuries and the linking theories and sociological relations.

Thesis

This article is about the theories that explain the differences in [my personal] family life and romantic relations between the 20th and 21st centuries and how they relate to the actual differences in examples (Real, 2007; Kendall, 2013b; Kendall, 2013a; Karthik786, 2013; Thompson, 2015). The theories can be read in the sections below (Real, 2007; Kendall, 2013b; Kendall, 2013a; Karthik786, 2013; Thompson, 2015).

ARTICLE 7

Differences in romantic relations and family life

Married life in the 20th century could be said to have been based on greater romantic companionship than in the 21st century (Real, 2007). This trend was because women needed to be dependent more on their husbands due to restrictions and the lack of representation for them (Real, 2007). Romantic relations after marriage in the 21st century can be described more as intimate love due to the increased dominance of the woman in her marriage role (Real, 2007). The theory of Intimate Marriage states that the five domains (the intellectual, emotional, physical, sexual and spiritual) combine with companionate marriage to make it more like a lover's relationship (Real, 2007).

Family life in the (early) 20th century saw women functioning in a more dependent role at home while men worked outside the home environment, with parties happy with such arrangements (Real, 2007). This is less so in the 21st century, because people tend to have less satisfactory relations with each other (Real, 2007).

Functionalist Theories of family and socialization

The functionalist theory of family states that men and women who work together perform distinctive roles in a family in order to function (Kendall, 2013b). According to this theory, a family is like an organism and each aspect of the family is like an organ that works together to keep the whole functioning smoothly, with family members, for example, working in occupations to contribute to society and studying in order to prepare for a working life (Kendall, 2013b).

The functionalist theory of socialization states that society's requirements are fulfilled when both genders contribute to its requirements by cooperating as a whole (Karthik786, 2013).

Originally, more women worked by doing housework compared to men, but since the 21st century compared to the [early] 20th century, their dominance in romantic relations and family lives is to be expected (Karthik786, 2013).

ARTICLE 7

Postmodernist Perspective Theory

For the 21st century, the Postmodernist Perspective theory of culture needs to be looked at (Thompson, 2015). This is based on the thinking that rapid social change has a negative impact on others through increased industrialisation and globalization, reducing the influence of social institutions as people begin to think less about others (Thompson, 2015). For example, decreased time spent communicating face-to-face with others is an effect of the loss of influence of social institutions on communication, which reflects the postmodernist perspective through industrialisation in communication (technology usage) (Thompson, 2015).

Industrialisation in communication is more prevalent in the 21st century than the 20th century (Thompson, 2015). As a result, people know and communicate more about and with each other through Facebook, Twitter and Google instead of face-to-face, and the loss of intimacy and recognition with face-to-face communication will worsen romantic relations and family life through loss of facial recognition and intimacy (Thompson, 2015).

The feminist perspective

The feminist perspective needs to be looked at regarding the differences in romantic relations and family life (Kendall, 2013a). This perspective states that social movements promoting the rights of women will improve them at the expense of men in romantic relations and family life (Kendall, 2013a). Women dominating over men in their relations is an action that reflects this perspective (Kendall, 2013a).

ARTICLE 7

Differences between my family members' lives between the 20th and 21st centuries

---

The theories above explain the differences in family life between the 20th and 21st centuries (Real, 2007; Kendall, 2013b; Kendall, 2013a; Karthik786, 2013; Thompson, 2015).

For example, my great-grandparents in the 20th century used to stay at home or the village nearby to work, with my great-grandfather working as an estate manager and my great-grandmother as a housewife. In the 21st century, my parents work as lawyers, although both are now retired. Their more westernized lifestyles [such as usage of technology] compared with my great grandparents' lifestyles is another key difference between their lives. There have been more disagreements, compared to my great grandparents' relationship. Their lives are materially better, but they have a less agreeable relationship, and they have spent more time communicating with others on computerized devices when compared to my great grandparents.

Before retirement, they had less time to interact with each other due to office work, having to work more hours away from home. These differences reflect the postmodernist and feminist perspectives besides the functional theory of family (Real, 2007; Kendall, 2013a; Thompson, 2015).

Based on the psychological theories mentioned above, one may expect my family to have less companionate parents in love and therefore, be less likely to stay functional (Real, 2007; Kendall, 2013a; Thompson, 2015).

REFERENCES

Collected Articles

Karthik786 (2013) Marriage and Love- From a Sociological Perspective.
[Online]. Available from: https://tinyurl.com/59j7hdey
[Accessed 26 June 2017].

Kendall, D. (2013a) Boundless Alternative to Sociology in Our Times: The Essentials, 9th Edition, Boundless.com.
[Online]. Available from: https://tinyurl.com/3wadxfn9
[Accessed 27 June 2017].

Kendall, D. (2013b) Boundless Alternative to Sociology in Our Times: The Essentials, 9th Edition, Boundless.com.
[Online]. Available from: https://tinyurl.com/fbtrwt3j
[Accessed 26 June 2017].

Real, T. (2007) 20th century vs 21st century marriage.
[Online]. Available from: https://tinyurl.com/ymxskvz4
[Accessed 28 June 2017].

Thompson, K. (2015) The Postmodern Perspective on The Family.
[Online]. Available from: https://tinyurl.com/338xz3z6
[Accessed 28 June 2017].

ARTICLE 7 - References

www.ingramcontent.com/pod-product-compliance
Lightning Source LLC
Chambersburg PA
CBHW071508220526
45472CB00003B/950

* 9 7 9 8 3 4 5 2 6 4 4 1 6 *